UNKNOWN TO MILLIONS!

UNKNOWN TO MILLIONS!

by

Steve Barclay

edited by
Bernard Bale
(Encore! Magazine)

Bookaholics Publishing, 2020.

Published by Bookaholics Publishing
imprint of
Estuary Media Group Ltd
19, Carters Garth Close, Grainthorpe, Louth,
Lincolnshire, LN11 7HT

ISBN: 978-1-9160289-7-5

Page design by Pageset Ltd, High Wycombe, Buckinghamshire HP11 1JR.
Printed by Ridgeway Press, Easton Royal Pewsey, Wiltshire SN9 5LU.

Contents

Dedication

Dedicated to my Mother, Beatrice Hutchinson

*Without her encouragement and support
I wouldn't have made it as far as the
Onward Hall Deansgate Manchester*

Foreword

by
INTERNATIONAL MEGASTAR
RICK WAKEMAN

In 2001 I was asked by Roy Hudd, to play Abanazar in the pantomime Aladdin at the Hall for Cornwall in Truro. I am a total pantomime groupie but had never been in one before and was nervous to say the least as I was well aware that pantomime is one of the most difficult of theatre productions to pull off successfully.

I expressed my concerns to both Roy Hudd, (the author), and Ian Liston from Hiss and Boo, but they said I was not to concern myself as there were some seasoned pantomime stalwarts who would guide me through , especially Steve Barclay who was playing Widow Twanky.

I arrived in November for the rehearsals having learned ALL my lines. At the first read through all the others had their scripts and Steve pulled me to one side and said…"You've learnt it haven't you"?…and I proudly replied "Yes".

"Wrong" , he said, "the scripts going to change massively so we only learn our lines after the changes have been made . It's really hard to unlearn , but you're going to have to do that"……and how right he was…but it was made easier by the hours that Steve spent with me going over lines and scenes we had together and he was far and away the finest pantomime dame I had ever seen . He was hilarious because he took the part seriously and the kids and parents loved him......as indeed did I.

Throughout that run we spent a lot of time together both on stage and off , and became great friends. Steve was always generous with his time and when a charity performance was organised to raise money for the local hospital he was the first to come forward and volunteer his services and do his musical hall act...which brought the house down.

We have remained friends ever since and I was extremely proud when he was rightly accepted o join The Grand Order of Water Rats where he has continued to help in raising thousands for well deserving charities.

As Ken Dodd rightly said..."You get a load of performers all rolled into one with Steve Barclay"...and never a truer statement was ever made and like many of us in the entertainment industry, I am proud to be able to call Steve a true friend. He is a credit to the business we all love.

Rick Wakeman

Overture

Steve's the name

Steve's the name – showbusiness is the game
It can drive you crazy – but that's the price of fame!

Actually there is a lot more to it than that and let say right from the start that although fame seems to have come in the form of being a Dame, that is only one string to my humble bow.

There is a great fascination in how a normal bloke can feel comfortable in putting on a frock. Some of the greatest entertainers have hated it – Sid James used to grit his teeth and get on with it if he had to dress as a woman for a Carry On scene; Ronnie Barker was also uncomfortable if he had to slip into a frock and Oliver Hardy positively loathed it.

Me? Well, I have been involved in laughter throughout my show business life and to me it is just another comedy costume – a clown outfit if you like.

Mind you, when I first found myself deciding which bra to wear, my face was so red you could have toasted bread on it!

Of course, being a Dame is only one of the many elements of show business I have tackled, enjoyed and sometimes even been successful with.

A lot of people have enjoyed what I do but I am still Unknown to Millions. That is so true of a lot of us.

Hope you like the title – Unknown to Millions – it was actually coined by Reg Thomson who was a brilliant comedy actor from Middlesbrough and played alongside people like Benny Hill on TV and films but was also rarely out of stage work ranging from dramas to panto.

Reg was one of those people who everyone knew by face but not so many by name, hence his stating that he was Unknown to Millions!

As for me well, let us not jump ahead. I'll tell you how it all started.

Are you sitting comfortably?......

CHAPTER ONE

Bitten by show business – how I slipped into the spotlight

Nivea cream is how I came into the business I just slipped in! ... I had better explain before you start making it up yourselves.

As a small boy of six or seven I was allowed to watch The Black and White Minstrel Show on our black and white telly from Radio Rentals. It was a fantastic production by George Mitchell and hugely popular throughout the land with massive viewing figures and many spin-offs in live theatre.

I loved watching the show, glued throughout to every song, every dance and every bit of comedy. I was so smitten that it inspired me to imitate this great BBC show in my playtime and try to copy everything I had watched.

The Nivea cream? Well, I was only a little lad at the time so make allowances but I would look around the house for some Nivea and while nobody was looking I would put some around my mouth and eyes and look at my face in the reflection of the telly screen. That was just the start because I would then sing Al Jolson songs to Torchy our Tom Cat. I did all the actions too. Torchy was long-suffering and would sit there with eyes half-closed and ears turned away as much as possible. When I spread my arms in Jolson style though Torchy was looking for the exit and demanding his money back.

Torchy was a hard audience but it was part of my very early show business education. "Entertain your audiences, don't frighten

1

them half to death" I learned another lesson too, if you can't find the Nivea don't try the Germolene instead – it makes your eyes water!

Those were indeed the early days and I had a fairly happy childhood, due in no small way to my mum and Dad who did their best to fight off the feelings of depression and loss that a personal tragedy could so easily have overwhelmed them. They worked hard to give our family the things we needed in life but not just material things. I'll explain.

They experienced one of the worst things any couple go through – a terrible tragedy losing their then youngest son Peter in a road accident. I think Peter must have been about five or six when he was killed and he would have been one of my older brothers, along with Trevor, or maybe not because I arrived on doctor's orders.

The grief and hurt was about to rip the family unit apart when my Mum, Beatrice, went to speak to the doctor for help. He advised that while they would never forget Peter they had to try and focus on the futrure and perhaps add to their family again! That's when I was born then eleven months later my sister Elaine.

So my parents performed wonders to look after us but never forgot Peter and, though we never met, neither have I.

That is where and why I began then. Little Steve Barclay was born on March 4th 1956 and christened Stephen Hutchinson. I am told that my then big brother Trevor was very proud of his new baby brother. I hope so, I was always proud of him.

Growing up during the 1950s and 60s was just great. I know that it is customary to say that I had an awful childhood full of problems but I didn't. We were an ordinary working-class family and there was never much money to spare but we were okay. I never had holes in my socks for very long and I was never sent up chimneys to earn some money.

From my earliest memories I knew I was destined for a showbiz career. Why? Well, from an early age I started to organise shows in our garden shed. It was not a particularly big shed but I have played worst venues since then!

I was always the main act of course I had support acts, thanks to Susan Calclough, Shirley and Janice Bright, my sister Elaine, Rusty the dog and, if we could catch him, Torchy our tom cat. What a bill! What a show! Our audiences were usually local kids and they could be relied upon to clap and cheer in all the right places. On reflection it was the early days of my expressing myself and finding an outlet for the show business heart that was beating inside me so early in life.

There must have been some influences and I don't think we need to look much further than Blackpool, the mecca of summer holidaymakers and the entertainment capital of Britain's seaside resorts.

In the 1960s we used to often go and stay in guest houses for a few days or a week. We love to be beside the seaside of course and there was always so much to see and do. I have always liked seaside rock as well – and I still have my own teeth, mostly! The biggest attraction of them all was of course, the summer shows and my Mum and Dad always made sure we saw the theatre presentations of the day. I remember seeing a young Jimmy Tarbuck along with Mike and Bernie Winters at the North Pier. We all loved comedy of course so seeing the great Arthur Haynes was a real thrill. When i think about it, I was so privileged to see stars like Tessie O'Shea, Matt Monroe, Winifred Atwell, The Bachelors, Mark Winter and a host of other great variety legends.

My Mum was like me – star struck but it was hard to get a glimpse behind the scenes of what seemed then the secretive world of show business. One Sunday night we ventured down the North Pier Blackpool to see On With The Show, a great seaside special with 1950s radio star Jack Storey. I think it was some kind of a more relaxed show due to 'performance rules of the day' as Jack seemed to be on and off all night, doing his famous landlady and postman routines. He did have some support acts but he also included in the show a talent section – they were very popular in those days – and also a give away slot – also very popular.

I remember it as if it as yesterday and I wish it was because Jack asked for talented volunteers. That was the start of another chapter in my life as you might well have guessed by now. Yes, I went up on stage and sang 'Yesterday' to tremendous polite applause by the enthusiastic holiday audience.

It was a major milestone for me. At last we were going to get that glimpse behind the curtains. We were finally invited into a proper theatrical dressing room with make-up and the lot! They say the smell of grease paint does something to you. Believe me, it does. I can recall the whole experience very vividly but if I couldn't, one thing I would definitely remember was the smell of the grease pain. From that first smell of it I was totally intoxicated. I have been addicted to it ever since and that first encounter with grease paint will live with me forever. Even now I might be clearing some old make up box and I get a whiff of On With The Show and that first meeting with my pal-to-be, Jack Storey.

As we left that Blackpool end of the pier show and its stars that evening, this eight-year-old boy was totally in a trance. I could not help keep on thinking, 'What I would give to perform here'. Eventually I did of course but more about Blackpool's North Pier and its theatre later in this book.

Back home in Oldham the weather was still warm enough to venture into the shed at the bottom of our garden, I rigged some old curtains up of my Mums, sorted myself the number one dressing room and that was it – we had our show. It was not like Blackpool but it as certainly pretty close to it in my mind.

One day my Mum came home and there we all were doing our show in full make up obtained from an old hand bag of hers. We had found the best Woolworths-could-buy Yardley foundation with a soft Rimmel pencil. It was probably quite grotesque rather than showbiz. What a way to start a career!

One Saturday afternoon my Mum called me and said, "Stephen it's Mother's day tomorrow and as your Dad's in America I am going to treat myself to a night out." I was a bit disappointed. I did not mind my Mum having a night out but I always liked ti best when we were all together. My face lit up though when she added, "But you and Elaine are invited to come with me."

The night out was not just a stroll to the fish and chip shop. My Mum Beatrice taking Elaine and I to see The Sasha Distel Show at the Gaumont. Manchester. The Gaumont was a big cinema and theatre which could seat just under 2,500 people and had been built on the site of the historic Hippodrome Theatre.

After our bus ride to the city centre from our home in Oldham we soon arrived at the theatre and it was Show Time! I was about 12 years of age at this stage and totally in 'wonderland' whenever I went to a theatre.

During the interval I made an excuse that I needed the toilet. It was an excuse but I just wanted to try and see something of behind-the-scenes. In fact I found a lift which in addition to circle, balcony, and stalls also had the word basement on one of the buttons. Well, being just twelve years old and very star struck, I couldn't resist it. I pressed basement.

When the left stopped and I arrived at the basement I found ice cream and other general usherette type stuff in a bit of a heap by the door. I duly crawled over it all and after walking through a series of passages I found myself strolling into the dressing room of another star – Ted Rogers, one of my heroes. I couldn't believe it and just froze and stared at him. I remember very well on his dressing table was a piece of course sponge full of makeup.

Ted looked at me and with a slight smile said, "Oh hello young man ... how can I help?"

I explained how I had come via the under passageway to try and meet him. I told him that I was a big fan as I had seen him lots of times on TV. I then went on to say that I wanted to be in show business.

Ted patiently listened and then replied, "Okay, well I'm very pleased to meet you young man. Would you like a photo?" I couldn't believe my luck but I quickly said, "Wow! Thanks!" Once he had signed a photo and presented it to me, Ted then took me to meet Sasha Distell and Stephane Grappelli. As it was mother's day the next day there were flowers in the dressing rooms of Sasha and Stephane. Ted then duly took me to the stage door and I think an usher took me back to where I should have been. It was another amazing experience and only fuelled my desire to be an entertainer.

If you don't mind, let us now fast forward to about six months before Ted Rodgers passed away in 2001 and I had been booked to appear at the Leeds City Varieties in their Music Hall weekend.

I was delighted to find that Ted was top of the bill.

The show's chairman and producer was Johnny Dennis and he took me to Ted's dressing room to introduce me to the star of the show. I shook Ted's hand and said, "You know Ted, we always meet in dressing rooms."

He looked a little vague but obviously didn't want to be impolite so I rescued him by explained that I was the cheeky little kid all those years ago who gate-crashed his dressing room when he did the Sasha Distell Show in Manchester.

"Yes, yes, yes," he said. "I remember that well!" He meant it too.

During that engagement Ted watched me work every night and then on the Saturday said, "Come and have a coffee with me Steve. I have a few things to say to you."

Sure enough, we had coffee and he dissected my act and gave lots of good advice. One thing he said was, "Steve why do you come on stage pushing a pram with a uke in it?"

I answered that I did it so that the uke was the payoff to the act and a surprise!

"Wrong," said Ted and went on to explain, "I worked with George Formby years ago. He always started his act with the uke, did some other stuff in the middle, then ended with the uke."

It was good advice and, well you've guessed it, that is what I do now and have done ever since Ted Rodgers took the trouble to give me some free advice… Thanks Ted!

CHAPTER TWO

How I got the key to the wonderful world of pantomime

I was totally smittten by the theatre and especially by variety but little did I know when I was taken to those shows in my very early years that there was still more magic to come. I had not yet seen my first pantomime.

I think I was about eight years old when my Mum and Dad told me that we were going to the panto. I vaguely knew what a pantomime was of course but I was still unprepared for the wonderful experience that was waiting for me at the Oldham Empire.

The legendary Joseph Locke – he made a come-back some years later as the mystery singer, Mr X – was appearing at the Empire in Aladdin. For those who don't know Joseph Locke he was an amazing tenor who totally captivated his audiences, sold thousands of records and was just a massive star. For him to be topping the bill at Oldham was just beyond belief, a real coup for the theatre.

The panto formula was much the same then as now. The bigger shows had one or more established stars to pull in the crowds just like they do today. It was a little different because the stars of those days were entertainers. Now it seems that sports stars who can't act, sing or dance, celebrity chefs or contestants from Big Brother will do, just so long as there is some connection with television. I know that sounds a but grumpy and some of those people turn out to be really good. There are many who don't though and they

7

have to be carried by the support cast who not only do their own jobs but try their best to make these inexperienced stars look like stars, if you see what I mean. Oh well, that's show business!

Anyway, there we were sitting in the theatre at Oldham and at last the house lights dimmed and the music began to play. There was an excited buzz and then a hush from the audience. The magic began. The pantomime started and it was great but there was no sign of Joe. Where was he? We began to wonder. Mum kept calm and just munched her chocolates. "Maybe he's not going to appear after all, he's dodging the tax man again."

I didn't have a clue what she was talking about but, unknown to me, Josef Locke was not only an amazing singer but he had also been in the news for allegedly evading paying taxes. My Dad kept the faith and said, "Keep quite Beatrice, there's time yet!"

Well, the show continued and I was enjoying it. The comic told his gags with the kids and the villain took the principle girl into his cave with the Dame warning her, "Don't take any toffees." We all laughed but the grown-ups seemed to be laughing on a different level to us kids. It was the end of the first half and still no Joe!

The interval came and a friend of my Father who was connected with the Theatre met us in the stalls.

My Mum, always being the sort that said what she was thinking, asked, "Where's Joe then?" The friend simply laughed and replied, "Oh, don't worry. He's on soon," He then asked if the kids would like to pop backstage for a few minutes and meet the panto comic.

We all answered before Mum or Dad had the chance. "Yes please!" So off we all went.

All the family wound our way via the velvet lined Exit doors and finally we found ourselves back-stage. If she had had any chocolates left my Mum would have choked on them as she stammered, "Oh look, it's him!"

We all peered and there was the man himself, Josef Locke. He was standing outside his dressing room wearing a black evening suit which looked a little strange since everyone around him was in Aladdin costume. They were straight out of the Arabian Nights and he was straight out of the Royal Albert Hall!

Mum didn't hesitate and said, "Now that's the autograph you want our Stephen, a proper star he is. Go on, ask him."

I think she was a bit in love with him, on a truly Woman's Own basis of course.

Joe signed our autograph books, and even gave us his black and white picture. I have treasured that to this day because he was not only a great star but it is such a great memory of my first ever panto experience.

My sister is called Elaine, and in the second half of the show right after the tabs opened, there was a stool on stage, and on walked Joe himself.

He sang a few songs, told some gags, and then shocked us by saying. "...And now a little song dedicated to Beatrice, Stephen, and Elaine – oh and their Dad of course..."

My mum nearly wet herself! After he had done his act, the panto went on – I do not recall him being in the finale though. Years later I told this story to the impresario Aubrey Philips whom I worked for in my very first pantomime. He said "Wow! That was my show! Small world. Aubrey and I are still in touch and always put the theatre world to rights.

I've learned that my great-great uncle was a musical director at the Oldham Empire years and years ago, and it's rumoured he taught George Formby how to clog dance – would that be old or young George? My great great uncle's name was John Mealier! If he rings any bells with anyone I would love to hear about him.

Since those theatre visits I have appeared in lots of pantomimes myself both as Comic and Dame, and I feel sure that it was that first sniff of the grease-paint at the Oldham Empire was the final spark that lit this passion I have for theatre and show business. Once it has bitten you, you might as well give in to it because you will never overcome it.

I think its true to say that there was always a pleasant odour when the tabs opened, it might be down to all the little preparations we do before curtain up, the deodorant spray after-shave and so on. Let's be honest though it was certainly none of those things in those days, the 'good old days' of variety. It was the old five and nine make up. It had a smell all of its own. They called it five and nine because the old liechener sticks had numbers and No 5 and No 9 made a nice flesh colour. Even at an early age I didn't know what it was but everyone on stage seemed to have great skin with a healthy glow, even the comedians. I was not to know until later that this was in fact their make up!

Those were the days! Oh, come on Steve, be honest. All right then – yes, I still use it!

During my time as a pantomime performer I have not looked back that often, but when I do it is hard to imagine that more decades than I care to admit have passed since that first wonderful pantomime experience and meeting the great Joseph Locke.

That was it for me, I knew I had to be on stage. I knew I had to entertain. I knew I wanted to be a part of that magic that had thrilled me so much. I knew I could do it too. I know it was a bit of a cheek but I felt that I could be up there alongside the comic, the Dame and the star. Little did I know that one day I would be all three.

Yes, I had the cheek, I had an amazing desire and I wanted nothing more than to be on the stage rather than looking at it. But how? I have been asked that question so many times – How do I start?

Well, that was the question dangling before my eyes and making my brain itch and my heart twitch.

How do I start?

It sounded very difficult but in fact it was a little easier then than now because the opportunities for live entertainment were so much greater. Today it is not unusual for someone to appear on television, get a following and then create an act. When I was starting out it was completely the opposite. You got an act, got some bookings and if you were very fortunate an agent, a manager or perhaps a show or TV producer would be in the audience one night and your talent was spotted, as they say.

That was all very well but first of all you had to have something to offer and then you had to actually convince someone to give you a chance.

One of the best chances of getting the early bookings was to get in touch with an agent who was booking acts for working men's clubs. You were never going to be a star over night and it was going to be hard work. Some nights you would be coming off stage walking on air but most nights you would come off stage and hope that the car would start – and as quickly as possible.

It was a roller-coaster ride but thank goodness for the clubs.

CHAPTER THREE

The clubs, the TV show and the dreams

T he great Northern clubs are a legend. There was no
halfway house with them. You either came out of there
thinking that you were ready for the London Palladium
or you felt that you were never going to appear in front of an
audience again. I know of one comedy act – two brothers – who
felt so awful when they came off that they climbed out of the loo
window and ran for it without even waiting to be paid. That's
what the working men's clubs can do for you.

If you get the chance to talk to anyone who used to work them
they will tell you all sorts of stories. Sometimes the dates were for
Sunday lunchtimes and you would find yourself playing to a load
of newspapers. It was strange that they just went to the club for a
pint and to read the paper and then as one they would empty out
to go home because they knew their Sunday roast would be on
the table. You sometimes wonder why you had been booked but
at least you get paid and you got the chance to read the front and
back pages of the newspapers while you were working.

You got some great introductions from the club secretary as
well.

Just before the next turn, a young man who says he's going to
make you laugh, I wanted you to know that our dear member
Percy Longbottom has just died. His widow has been on the phone
and wants to know if anyone wants to buy his pigeons......

Before the next act, the committee wants to apologise to you for the rubbish act we had last week. The agent has said that he thinks this one will be better but if not we can have our money back......

They also love trying to turn you into a star by telling everyone where you have been appearing.

This next lad comes to us for the first time. He was at the Talk of The Town, Cleckheaton last week so I should think he'll be all right...

Others get more enthusiastic. Some even want to be comics themselves.

We are delighted, ladies and gentlemen to bring you, at great expense, a young man who has come to us direct from the London Palladium. Yes, he was selling programmes there...

It was not always like that of course and if they wanted to make me sound like a star, they only had to look as far as television because by the time I was starting out on the clubs, I had been fortunate enough to appear on the then very popular Junior Showtime, a kids talent show which was on ITV. How did I manage that? Audacity! Let me explain.

Does anyone remember Radio Rentals? Well, as I mentioned before, we got our television from there, a black and white idol which sat on a throne in the corner of the room and was a magical magnet when it was switched on and my dressing room mirror when it was switched off. I had never forgotten every detail of those backstage dressing rooms I had seen and the TV seemed to be perfect to play that role in my imagination.

I was still a kid of course and used to run all the way home from school so that I didn't miss Blue Peter. Even at that young age I had an eye for the ladies and especially Valerie Singleton. I also used to love ITV's Magpie and Susan Stranks. I hadn't quite made my mind up which one I was planning to marry when I grew up but the matter was under consideration. I was not even put off by the fact that I never did get a Blue Peter badge. Perhaps that was a good thing really because it is a well-known fact that if a lady gives you a Blue Peter badge you then have to marry them.

My modest sights at the time were on the girls at school and I quickly found that the way to their hearts was to make them laugh. It didn't really matter whether they laughed at you or with you, either way you got their attention and I seemed to be able to do that which also gained me the admiration of the other lads. I suppose I had become the class character.

Max Miller said that if you can make 'em laugh, the girls fall at your feet and the guys want to shake your hand. He was right and that still applies today unless of course, you are interrupting a serious relationship in which case the girl might fall at your feet but the guy will want to shake you by the throat!

Anyway, it worked at the time when I was at school and I had a pal called Eddie Bainbridge who used to suggest jokes and one-liners to me. I had already started doing impersonations in the playground and Eddie used to say, "Next time you do your Harold Wilson impersonation why not say this......or that." Yes, Eddie was my first comedy script writer and with his suggestions I soon had an "act" doing impressions of David Frost, Harold Wilson and Ken Dodd. I suppose my act lasted for all of three minutes but it was a start and I did it quite often at school and also at home.

I ought to tell you at this stage that there was another television programme that i would have run all the way round the planet to see – Junior Showtime! This was basically a talent show for kids and produced by Yorkshire Television. It was brilliant and I used to watch every second of every show. Bobby Bennett presented the show, a very talented all-rounder and among the others who appeared as kids were Joe Longthorne, Lisa Stansfield, Pauline Quirke, Bonnie Langford, Malandra Burrows, Mark Curry and others who went on to greater things. Glyn Poole of the then famous Poole Family, winners of Opportunity Knocks was a regular on the show. Opportunity Knocks? That's another story. It was like Britain's Got Talent only without so much glitter.

At the end of each Junior Showtime when they rolled the credits they also used to put the address to write to if you fancied having a go. I argued with myself for some time as to whether I should apply or not and in the end my audacity won the day and I wrote a letter to Junior Showtime, Yorkshire TV Centre, Leeds, LS3 1 JS. Yes, I can still remember it! Nobody at home was particularly surprised because they knew that show business was on my mind pretty constantly.

The real surprise came when an envelope arrived a little while later and excitement mounted because on that envelope was the YTV logo. The excitement soon died down though as the thought stepped in that it was a "thanks but no thanks" letter. There was only one way to find out and it was with shaking hands that I opened it.

Would I please attend an audition at The Onward Hall, Deansgate, Manchester! Would I! I certainly would! Then I read the next line – "Please bring sheet music as our pianist will be available." Sheet music? I had never thought of that! Where am I going to get sheet music? The panic set in and I had only just opened the envelope. Little did I know that I had just entered the real world of show business, a world of wonder, a world of comedy,song and applause, a world of PANIC!

I needed the music for Frost on Sunday and something like a chunk of Love Is like a Violin for my Ken Dodd impersonation.

My Dad was working abroad at the time so I could not expect him to help with the music and by the time I was due to appear at the audition, I still had no music. I had a new suit. I had a clipboard for my David Frost impersonation and I had a ticklin' stick for doing Doddy. I had my Mum with me as well but I had no music.

When I got there with a complete air force of butterflies re-enacting the Battle of Britain in my stomach I was relieved to find that the pianist was a kind-hearted chap and had seen all this "got no music" stuff before. He just smiled when I said, "Can you play dadada da dada?". He assured me that he could and that helped my butterflies to be a little less flappy. I don't know who he was but if the gentleman concerned is still around, please give me him my sincerest thanks for helping a 14-year-old who was in panic overdrive.

On the audition panel was a lady called Jean Pearce, a choreographer from Leeds and I heard not to long ago that she is still involved with dance. Apparently she tells people she has retired but in reality she is still as active. Jean was with Junior Showtime for six years and I wonder how many careers she helped launch in that time. She certainly played a part in launching mine.

My turn came and I did my stuff with the help of some new gags from Eddie Bainbridge, one or two a little near the knuckle for someone of my age but still acceptable for children's television. The panel seemed to enjoy what I did but I came away not knowing if I had done enough to impress them into giving me a chance on the show. All I got was a rather bland, "We'll be in touch."

You can imagine that I became a postman stalker for the next few days and lived permanently with disappointment when nothing arrived. To be honest I have daily met the postman with both dread and hope ever since. The dread is of another bill while the hope is for a long-awaited cheque or contract. I wonder if postmen know how much they mess with our minds? Seriously, I have aways appreciated postmen, out in all weathers, running the gauntlet of dogs, taking the blame for bad news. I wonder how they protect themselves from all this – perhaps they wear chain mail!

Anyway, the letter finally arrived. Could I be at the YTV studio by 8 am to record Junior Showtime? It said that we would need to organise a permission licence from the education authorities and also said that they would meet all expenses. Wow! I was almost a professional!

My Mum rang my Dad in America. We had a party line in those days. Do you remember them? You used to share the line with someone else and if they were on the phone you couldn't use it. Our number was 0161-633-0121. Why is it that you can always remember the useless things but can't remember where you put your keys?

My mum also told all the neighbours and phoned the Oldham Chronicle who came straight away to do an interview and take a photo. I still have the clipping actually.

At last the big day arrived in January and my butterflies travelled with my Mum and I on the train to Leeds, into the taxi to the YTV studios and finally into the reception area of the great building. Funnily enough the nearer we got to the studio the more the butterflies became agitated but once into that reception area they settled down. It was almost as if I felt at home there straight away.

It was not long before a tall, slim man wearing a polo neck

sweater came into view. He walked up to us, smiled and introduced himself. He was Mike Bevan, the producer and he gently ushered us to a dressing room and then to the canteen where we were provided with an excellent breakfast.

We had just finished eating when Mike re-appeared and asked, "Could you come into the studio please, Les would like to meet you all."

We did as we were asked of course but couldn't help wondering who Les was. We soon walked into the studio and I was struck right away by the bright lights and the smell of fresh paint.

This chap who wanted to meet us was in the centre of the studio chatting away with people and putting them all at ease. Of course, he was none other than Les Dawson and I was thrilled when he spoke to me and asked me what I did. He listened intently and said, "I bet you're funny, aren't you." I just said that I hoped so. I think he was in Leeds appearing in panto as Dame. Dame? Yes, Les was one of the greatest Dames ever but more of that later in the book.

Finally we went through our routines in a kind of rehearsal and when I finished Mike said to Jean that he thought we might need to call in Bert. Who was Bert? I had discovered who Les was but now there was another name to get to know.

Bert turned out to be Bert Gaunt, comedy advisor to Junior Showtime. After about an hour he arrived and introduced himself. He was very kind and helpful and suggested that I should change some of the material for my Harold Wilson impersonation. He gave me this gag (imagine the Harold Wilson voice if you can) – "Somebody asked me what, if I get back in office, I am going to do for the little man...well, I'll tell you – I'm going to get him a little woman!"

I tried it and it worked beautifully. In fact Bert told me to leave the rest as it was so I did and the rest of the day went brilliantly. We met Diana Dors, Tony Carlton and all the cast from Queenie's Castle which was a very popular TV show at the time. We also met Freddie Fletcher, star of the classic film Kez and we also met a jobbing actor who was also from Oldham. His name? Roy Barraclough!

It really was an amazing day and when we finally got home I found it really hard to sleep that night. I was tired out but I could not stop reliving everything that had happened.

That was not the end of it though as the show had been recorded and was not due for trannsmission until a long six months afterwards.

Of course we were glued to the television on the evening it actually appeared and I was thrilled to see the end product. I wasn't really prepared for what happened next though.

The following day I boarded the No7 bus at Limeside to go to school and everyoone applauded. I spent the journey signing autographs. It was actually quite embarrassing although I must confess that I did enjoy it. After school we had to go into town to Boots the Chemist and a lot of the assistants also asked for autographs. I could not believe the reaction to my appearance on Junior Showtime but my feet firmly landed back on the ground when we got on the No 426 bus to go home. Nobody gave me a second glance let alone ask for an autograph. That was when I realised that fame is short-lived and certainly has its casualties.

But it was great while it lasted.

Perhaps this would be a good time to introduce an old pal of mine, Chris Whatmough. He got in touch while we were writing this book and told me that he had done a bit of a write-up on me. Telling a little of my story from someone else's point of view seemed like a good idea so here's a brief memory from Chris.

"I met Steve at Grange Comprehensive School in Oldham when we both joined the same class at the age of around 14 years old. I am sure that Steve would not mind me saying that he was an outgoing young man who with his chatty personality and twinkling eyes knew how to attract attention. This he did in the most entertaining style by impersonating others including teachers. Talk about taking your life into your own hands! Believe me, those teachers (being polite because I could find other ways to describe them), had no sense of humour and would issue severe punishments like beating you with a leather strap whilst holding a smile on their faces for such cheek. Oh yes, happy days (that's a joke folks!)

It was probably because of this misery that Steve was such a breath of fresh air. Some days he would gather a group by his witty impersonations of celebrities and politicians of the day and other he would produce a banjo uke and do the most convincing impressions of George Formby whilst playing in a truly professional style. I think one day he changed the words of "Our Sergeant Major" to the name of a school teacher which went down well.

After some time, Steve was quite well known in school for his entertainments and there was an air of excitement when we found out that he was auditioning for Junior Showtime, a television showcase programme for young performers. I know that his attitude to entertaining had by this stage changed from one of larking around to a more committed and focused approach and whilst it was difficult for me to understand Steve at that time, I do with hindsight believe he had then got the bit between his teeth and could smell a career in entertainment.

Certainly I was going around telling all my family, aunts, uncles, next door neighbour etc. that my mate was going to be on't telly. The show went out and to see someone you knew on tv in those days of only three channel's was a big thing. In my mind I can see him now stood there in a Ganex raincoat doing the impression of Harold Wilson smoking a pipe saying "there'll never be another"

Steve was now getting work entertaining in the clubs and pubs, making a name for himself and so as to speak serving his apprenticeship whilst still at school. That was impressive to any kid like me!

My mother would for years after relate the story of Steve visiting our home when we were still at school to entertain playing the banjo uke. She never forgot! Not long before my Father died at the grand old age of 93 earlier this year, we were watching a video of George Formby – No Limit, when he asked part way through the film, "what ever happened to Steve Hutchinson". Yes, he remembered Steve all those years on.

I clearly recall one lunchtime sitting on a croft near to school, on a hot summer's day, smoking fags with Gary Travis, Jimmy Stonier and Terry Ward and talking about what we were going to do next now that we were about to leave school and get jobs.

I remember discussing Steve Hutchinson and his plans to leave school and go directly into entertainment and admiring him for having ambition but at the same time wondering whether he would achieve his dreams when in reality most young kids then only aspired to some other more mundane career. I went home from that meeting and discussion never to return to Grange School and never to see Steve, Gary, Jimmy or Terry again. That was my last day at school!

Today, some 43 years on, I take pleasure in looking back at Steve's formative years and now knowing that he achieved his dream and continues to do what gives him most happiness – entertain!"

Thanks Chris, cheque's in the post! This could start to seem like This Is your Life! So I had better get on with it.

CHAPTER FOUR

My Blackpool debut – and a 'proper job'

Where was I? Nowhere near being a Dame just yet but I was experiencing short-lived fame. My teen years continued almost normally for a while. I spent a lot of time with my friends in Limeside on various adventures, either at Daisy Nook or Bill Bennet's farm over by Roman Road. Bill Bennet was never seen by us kids, but later in my life I was to admire Billy Bennet the Music Hall comedian all because of a meeting with Roy Hudd in Paignton Devon many years in the future. However Limeside was built in the 1950's on 'farm land' so there were still lots of meadows stiles and fields available as yet untouched by 1950's Britain. Perfect for my friends and I to explore. All this and in-between time trying to get an act together in front of the large mirror in my bedroom.

Don't forget as yet I had no income to support the purchase of the props I would need for this brilliant act of the future! However, I did have a small tape recorder (reel to reel) that my Dad had brought back from America in the 60s. I remember vividly the small disc-like pink and gold microphone in my hand. Put a microphone in the hand of an entertainer – or would-be entertainer – and it is like putting a light to the blue touch-paper on a firework.

I used to get carried away with things like … "Ladies and Gentlemen, please greet the star of the show, Steve Hutchinson! And on the show tonight we have Rusty the Dog and the new cat

23

in town – Shandy!" I made many recordings like that, preparation for the great career I was hoping for but also a bit of fun at the time!'

After Junior Showtime it could all have been a bit of an anti-climax but little did I know that a new doorway to fame was just around the corner and someone had left it unlocked.

One day I was walking through the Tommy Field market in Oldham on my way home from school carrying my banjo uke. One of the market traders said, "Oi! Come here lad ... Is that a banjo your carrying? Can you play it?"

The banjo was out in a flash ... the market trader listened for a while, smiled and said, "Okay, stand there son and play until I tell you to stop!"

I played and sang some obscure George Formby song and the crowds wandered up to the trader's market stall. When he had a sizable crowd around his stall he gave me the eye to halt my performance. Reluctantly I did as he had asked. I was enjoying myself, I had an audience but not for long as the trader took over, seizing his chance to capture the crowd with his brilliant market trader and selling his pots and pans. After he had sold a large amount of his ware and the crowd was thinning he came over to me and gave me a crisp five pound note! The trader then said: "If you want to come Friday afternoon and all day Saturday then there is a job here for you Son."

I was delighted at being paid to perform and I turned up as requested Friday after school with a repeat of the performance but this time he only gave me three pounds as it had not proved so much of a draw. Oh well, that's show biz – my first 'if it show'. Saturday proved a hard slog because by this time I was expected to load the stall at around 7.00 am, go to the market café for the teas and breakfasts, play the uke as required, go for the dinners and then, at the end of the day, load the stock into the van. My wages were still three pounds! Maybe I was not cut out for 'Market life' after all. What I needed was an agent!

The next week with money in my pocket I set off on the bus to Manchester. Usually I got off the bus at Tip Street so that I could go into the many joke shops that lined the street at the time, I was innocent of the fact then but Tip Street was also a red light area. Had I known I might have been a bit quieter about where I wanted to get off, if you'll pardon the expression.

I would walk past the big shops like Lewis's, Affleck and Brown, Pauldens to Deansgate but would always have time to stop at second hand shops on the way looking for Ukes. I was no stranger to this trip around Manchester so in no time at all I was on Deansgate heading for Quay Street and the Granana TV studios. When I arrived at the reception I noticed Wilfred Pickles – remember him? – coming out to his taxi then right behind him was Johnny Hamp who was a big name in television and producer, among many things, of the massively-popular Comedians Show.

"Hello Mr Hamp," I stuttered, plucking up all my courage. "My name's Stephen Hutchinson and I want to be a comedian."

He very kindly stopped and spoke to me. "How old are you Stephen?" He asked. I told him that I was 15 and that I had been on Junior Showtime and many BBC radio shows. I told him I did clubs as well. That was not as unusual in those days as it might seem now. Johnny thought for a moment and said: "Mmmm... You need an agent son." With that he seemed to search in the depths of his jacket and eventually took out a card from his pocket and said: "There you are son, try this guy. I must go now." He wished me all the best and got into his taxi. I looked at the card which read: "HARRY GUNN – THEATRICAL AGENT" and included his address and phone number; I put the card in my pocket and made my way up to Arnolds Theatrical Shop and Mamalocks Music Shop, both of which were just a short walk back towards Deansgate. Needless to say I was excited and thought that the agent's card was like having a piece of gold in my pocket.

Arnolds Theatrical Shop was run by an oriental-looking lady who turned out to be Irish. To me she looked oriental because of her thick make up, coal black, scrapped back hair and long gown. I had been going into the shop for some time and had made quite a friend out of this lady. She told me about going to Paris in the autumn for all her masks and theatre wigs etc. She also told me her late husband was a magician who toured the world on cruise liners. This shop was so different from the joke shops on

Tip Street and felt much more like real show business. Everything had a place and the magic props and theatrical make up was kept under clean glass cabinets. It was also in a classier part of town.

I always visited Arnolds at around 4.00 pm, as that is when Mrs Arnold stopped for tea! On this day she said 'Oh I'm glad you have come Stephen I've been to Kendal's and bought some nice cream cakes for us'. I made several future trips to Arnolds and Mrs Arnold taught me about theatre make up and even gave me some theatrical teeth I use to impersonate Ken Dodd to this day. The teeth must be more than forty years old. When Mrs Arnold gave me the teeth from one of her class cabinets she told me "These will bring you luck … they are from Paris you know." Not many people are given lucky teeth as a present! No wonder I was bitten by show business!

Do not be misled, Mrs Arnold did not suffer fools. On many occasions I witnessed her throw out people who 'over browsed' as she called it and two big stars of the day, Hugh Lloyd and Terry Scott, were thrown out another reason!

Later that week I searched in my pockets but could not find the business card of Harry Gunn. I was really upset about that. His name was etched on my brain and I wondered if this could be the man who would hold key to my ambition of a successful theatrical career?

As my teen years were starting to roll by, in addition to doing the working mens clubs of Manchester I managed to get guest appearances on BBC's Junior Home Time and recorded a Christmas Special with a very young Lisa Stansfield from Rochdale. The presenter was a lovely chap, a sports editor called Tom Tyrell. Tom introduced me to Zena Sharpe Personal Management. Now Zena worked from a rather swanky house in Cheshire. She got me many auditions for TV parts including the part of Sandy Richardson in the massive1970's TV Soap Crossroads. Yes, I could have been THAT Sandy. What happened? Well, I failed all the auditions because I was so full of nerves and had developed a stutter. Great. Let's face it a stutter is not good news for any actor or performer but I got one that I hadn't had before. I couldn't tell "talk from stutter". Sorry about that, I have been the same since I was told that I had been brought by a Stork! Think about it, if you are old enough.

I remember doing an audition at Granada TV for some drama on one particular occasion because afterwards I went on 'walk about'. I walked through the set of Coronation Street and went into the corner shop, in the Rovers Return, up and down the street and in some of the houses. It was brilliant and and nobody stopped me as I walked with confidence and they assumed that I was meant to be there.

Anyway, I finally left school at 16 with a few GCSE's, about two of which were deemed as 'O' Levels as they were grade ones. They were science subjects and as we all know science uses formulas! I had purchased a brand new clear 12" ruler and on the flat side with a pin I scratched $I = V/R$ etc. etc. Then I scratched silly things on the other side. When flat on the desk it appeared an old ruler with Jane Luvs Jack etc. etc. on but turned over and tilted to the light it revealed all the formulas you needed to pass an O level exam! This was an elaborate ploy but was needed to gain an apprenticeship in those days. I knew I would own up one day and I take my punishment of writing a thousand lines or listening to the speeches of Tony Blair.

By this time I was already quite a local star in the clubs and pubs of Oldham and Manchester but I was not making enough money to warrant a career. One day my Dad looked me in the eye and said: Stephen, ring these up. This will be good for you." When I looked, hoping he had found someone wanting a new star, I was a bit disappointed to find that that the ad in the Oldham Evening Chronicle read: "WANTED – APPRENTICE FITTER. Apply to GEORGE SUMNER – OLDHAM."

I rang the number hoping that nobody would answer but someone did and to my surprise they asked me to go for an interview the next day. That evening I was taken through a rehearsal. While my Mum ironed my shirt for the next day, my Dad put me through a few spoof interviews and told me not to talk unless asked, take deep breaths for the stutter and FOR GOODNESS SAKE DON'T MENTION YOUR STAGE ACT!!!!

The next day I was on the bus and soon walking through the

engineering factory of George Sumner Ltd. It was around July time so the dock doors were wide open. A kindly man called Barry Caveny interviewed me and I got the job there and then. Barry told me that things had changed since his early working days and that they didn't send apprentices to the chippy or get them to make the tea.

They now send them to School. In my head I thought, 'Oh great. Thank you Harold Wilson and the trade unionists for such a caring thought' Back to school???!!!! Aaaarrrghhh!!!!

Since the job was to start in September I had July and August in which to dream about my showbiz career although knowing I was going to start an apprenticeship did keep my Mum and Dad happy. However while I was dreaming I got a temporary job in Alexandra's, a tailors Shop in Manchester. One day. during my break, I was walking past a men's boutique shop and a voice came out of the doorway "Hiya Steve, remember me?"

I did. It was Mike Constantia, a young guy who had once said that he wanted to be an agent. Many years later he did and I worked for him on club dates around Manchester. In fact as recently as last year I did a show for him.

My Mum was having a week in Blackpool in August with my Auntie Lilly so it was arranged that I would join them for a few days mid-week then go back home and look after Rusty our dog and Shandy the cat. Those few days in Blackpool made me realise even more what I really wanted to do with my life. Whilst my Mum and auntie were happy to go to Uncle Tom's cabin I was off in a different direction.

In the morning sun I headed down the golden mile to the North pier were I gazed at all the summer season posters. The big show that year was The Comedians with a handful of the star comics from the TV series including Frank Carson, Ken Goodwin, Bernard Manning, and Colin Crompton. I also noticed a poster which said Peter Webster's Talent Show in the Sun Lounge at 2.00 pm.

I could recognise Peter Webster by his small pencil moustache. As I stood there at about 11.00 am I suddenly saw him so I took a deep breath, went straight up to him and said. "Hello my name's

Steve Hutch and Johnny Hamp's sent me!"

Peter stopped in his tracks and without cracking his face said, "Johnny Hamp's sent you son. Ok, what do you want?"

I went on regardless. "Well he said that you may be interested in me for next year's summer season," I lied.

"Oh yeah ..." Peter had sussed me straight away of course but he played along with it. "Well why don't you enter the talent contest this afternoon?"

"Ok," I said, "I'll see you later."

There was a little cloud of dust as I sped off back to the bed and breakfast and grabbed my uke. That afternoon I was introduced by Peter as "from Oldham (there was a big cheer as it was Oldham Wakes week) STEVE HUTCH!"

I opened with a George Formby song, did a few impressions of the day and closed with another Formby song. I got great laughs and a great response but I still lost to an old lady who played the spoons.

As I walked away from the sun lounge with mixed feelings I heard an unexpected voice call "Hey Steve!" I thought it was Peter Webster who had forgotten to ask me to sign a contract for next year. But to my horror it was in fact Barry Caveny, company secretary of George Sumner Ltd to whom my Dad had expressly told me not to mention my show business act or dreams.

"I did not know we were having a talented apprentice in our midst Steve," said Barry. My stutter returned as I talked it down and said, "Well, it's just a bit of fun really, something I've always done Barry."

He shook my hand and said, "Very well done young man any road, see you soon." in his broad Oldham accent. I think Barry knew that I was not going to be 'apprentice of the year' at George Sumner Ltd but he was a kind man and kept my secret safe and at a distance from my new working life. I was relieved of course but could not get it out of my mind that I had felt so at home on stage at the Sun Lounge.

CHAPTER FIVE

A Star At Last…Well, Sort Of

So there I was in Blackpool having failed to win a talent contest but still in dreamland surrounded by the bright lights and the stars. I soon recovered from being rated less talented than an old lady playing spoons because after tea back at the B & B I had made my mind up that I was going to rub shoulders with the comics at the North Pier.

I could not afford a ticket so I wandered round to the stage door and asked for Colin Crompton who was one of those stars and a really popular Northern comedian.

The stage door keeper eyed me suspiciously and asked, "Who shall I say wants him?" I wasn't expecting that one so I took a breath, rushed a few thoughts through my head and blurted out: "Oh, tell Colin it's Harry Gunn from Manchester."

I was soon whisked up to Colin's dressing room and invited in after I knocked on the door with one hand and with my other fingers crossed behind me. Colin stood there in his dressing gown smoking a fag. He looked at me, raised an eyebrow and said, "Oh, not the Harry Gunn I was expecting."

Once I was inside the room I confessed my white lie and to me relief Colin just laughed and then said, "Ok how can I help you?

"I want to be a comedian on the North Pier Blackpool," I replied, waiting for a none-too-pleased response. Colin just smiled, gave me a programme and said, "Drop a line to Bernard Delfont, his address is on the programme. What have you got to lose except the price of a stamp?" Feeling much encouraged I thanked him, shook hands and then as I was about the leave the

31

room he added, "Oh yes, one other thing – don't tell him you are Harry Gunn, you'll be fired before you start."Colin could never pass up a chance for a joke. We both laughed and off I went with my mind racing and my emotions screaming at me. I had met one of my heroes and he had encouraged me. I had been backstage and I loved it.

I didn't sleep well that night, I was to excited but the next morning my Mum gave me some money so I went straight out and bought a matinee ticket to see Tessie O'Shea, Ronnie Ronalde, Joe Church, Bernie Clifton and Rod Hull & Emu. They were all appearing at the Winter Gardens. Little did I know that I had just bought a ticket to see some of the great entertainers with whom I would be working at later dates.

Tessie O'Shea was awesome and after the first show I was at the stage door of the Winter Gardens to try and meet her. I admit it, I was stagestruck but there was more to it than that – I just loved being in the theatre and among entertainers.

A tall man at the stage door looked at me without smiling and said: "Sorry young man but Miss O'Shea is not feeling very well so she won't be available to meet anyone. Now go home whoever you are."

Disappointed but undaunted I went into the car park and saw Tessie's vintage Rolls Royce.That told me that she must still be there so I thought I'll have another try. I went back into the theatre through another door and found my way through the many passages to the dressing rooms and literally bumped into Liverpool comedian Johnny Hackett who was doing a show with Cilla Black at the Blackpool Opera House.

Johnny was friendly and asked if he could help me. I explained how I wanted to see Tessie and tome surprise and delight he just said, "No problem, come with me."

He was great and introduced me to Tessie briefly and then I heard a voice from behind me, "It's that little sod again! This time go and don't come back, I'm ever so sorry Tess ... I think hes one of those nutters." Yes, it was the same man who had tried to put me off earlier and basically thrown me out. I would later find out he was in fact Frank Woodruff who was 'calling' the show and sent from the Forrester George Agency to 'look after all the artistes'.

For those who are not sure, "calling the show" means making sure everyone is on stage at the right time. There is a lot more to it than it might seem because someone 'calling' or looking after the show finds himself filling many other roles like arranging guest tickets, getting fresh bottles of booze and being there when a temperamental artiste is venting his spleen because the microphone went wrong.

Later in my career whilst doing a long summer season in Torquay with Danny La Rue, Frank Woodruff was introduced to me by Danny who said," This is Frank Woodruff, Steve. He's here to help us all. Anything you want he's the man, aren't you Frank?"

Frank beamed at me and said, "Oh yes, anything. Glad to meet you Steve. You're in dressing room No 2. Anything I can do, just ask luv."

Needless to say he had not recognised me but I had recognised him and I didn't ask for anything, luv."

Whilst working at ALCA ELECTRONICS I was also a young impressionist working the northern clubs I was so desperate to do pantomime but had no idea how to start the ball rolling. I worked for several managements in Manchester one of which was ACE Agency run by Clare De Castro known simply as Madame Ace. Madame Ace sounded rather grand over the telephone and as an agent she ran a small but good agency from her house in Cheatham Hill and occasionally would get me a last minute gig in Salford. She was a great old pro and had a son she called Pike? I would phone her about 7.30 Saturday evening and she would say, "Oh it's a bit flat tonight dear. It would probably be better if you just rehearse for next week." I remember her saying the same about Christmas Eve 1971.

One day Madame Ace rang me and said, "You know all this pantomime stuff you say you would like to do...Well, there's a man I know called Aubrey Philips who is looking for a Wolf in Red Riding Hood."

She went on to say, "Mr Philips would very much like to see you. Could you meet him at the Coliseum Theatre, Rhyl next Saturday/"

Of course, a big "Yes!" was the answer and a week later I was on the train from Manchester to Rhyl. I took the train that morning from Manchester Picadilly station clutching my suitcase full of props and my stage attire, I set off early so that I would be in plenty of time. I arrived at Rhyl station around 9.30 am for my 11.o'clock appointment. It was a freezing cold day so I went into a cafe and had a coffee, then went to the theatre. The Coliseum was a small round building right on the sea front. I waited and waited till it was almost dark there were no Aubrey Philips and no shelter from the cold and wind the Irish Sea offered. I caught my train back to Manchester, cold and feeling very dejected. When I arrived home my Mum and Dad were waiting for the news of my adventure, I was rather afraid to tell my Dad, wondering what he might say or do! The next day I telephoned Madam Ace and told her of my day's disappointment and this lady who was normally so softly spoken and rather posh just said, "The bastard!" She went on to say in no uncertain terms, "Leave this to me, I'll sort him out!"

I don't think I ever got any explanation for his rudeness but. not to be stopped by his non- appearance, another meeting was set up for the following week, I think Aubrey had to pay my train fare as recompense. So, the next Saturday I met Aubrey at the theatre. Again, I was there well before time looking at this round building thinking one day I will be doing my act in there. Aubrey took me for coffee then said, "Right then young 'un, let's go!"

"Where to?" I asked, "Back to the theatre for the audition?"

"No, no," replied Aubrey. "We need to go round to my friend's house. She has a piano." The next bit will live with me for the rest of my life as the strangest audition I have ever had.

We duly arrived at the lady's house and indeed she was a pianist, Aubrey said, "Well, have you any dots?"

"Dots?" I questioned Aubrey looked into the air and said, "Music!"

I changed in the kitchen and after making a proper entrance into the parlour proceeded to present my act – STEVE HUTCH, impressionist of tomorrow – in full dress suit, bow tie, the lot in this lady's front parlour. She brilliantly played all the right notes for the impressions of the day. Aubrey seemed impressed because I listened to his comments about my act.

Later that week Madam Ace rang to say that Aubrey was offering a six week run at the Library Theatre Luton followed by a six week tour of the provinces which included Oakengates, Tewksbury, etc. my fee was just £23 per week.

The strangest audition Aubrey ever did was told to me by Peter Darren, the Black and White Minstrel and lead singer whom I met in the pantomime. He recalled that Aubrey Philips, director of Philip Bernard Productions, had placed an ad in the stage asking for – 'pantomime artistes all lines – please phone Aubrey Philips on this number'. Peter duly rang from a phone box armed with a bag full of ten pence pieces. Aubrey picked up the telephone and said, "Hello. Philip Bernard Productions." Just then the telephone pips went (making that da da da sound we all knew in the 70s).

Pete,r calling from Southampton, put in another chunk of ten pence pieces and said, "Mr. Philips. I'm applying for the job as Prince in your pantomime..." (da da da da etc) puts more money in.

Aubrey said. "Ok, can you sing?" Peter, bemused by the question, replied, "Of course I can – I was in the Minstrels for years Mr. Philips."

Aubrey said, "Ok, sing then..."

Peter responded, "What here on the phone?" (da da da da etc.) He put more money in and then sang a few bars from the shows (da da da da etc.). Aubrey then said, "Ok, six weeks, Luton, £28 per week, the contract will be in the post." and put the phone down!

However, I got the same six week run at the Library Theatre Luton followed by a six week tour of the provinces which included Oakengates, Tewksbury, and so on and my fee was, as agreed. just £23 per week as Wolf with a comedy spot in the second half.

For this one moment of fame I ran away from home and an engineering apprenticeship at ALCA Electronics much to my father's disappointment! But this was it I'd made it to my first professional pantomime.

When the time arrived I boarded the Yelloway coach to Luton

with my banjo uke in a suit case with my impressionist props. It seemed like an eternity but we soon reach Luton I walked down the steps of the coach then heard that whoosh sound coaches make as the door closes. Then the coach sped off into the distance with my props and banjo uke in the boot! What would I do now ... A man at the office explained that the coach would not stop until Dunstable then would not pass by Luton until about 1.00 am the next day. When I arrived at my digs the owner said he would take me to pick up the coach at 1.00 am, how kind of him I thought. We picked up the suit case and got back to the digs by around 2.30am the house was dark and silent. I thanked the owner of the guest house for his trouble, to which he said 'Oh that's OK, but why don't you stay in my room tonight, but for now let me give you a little kiss'. Then he leaned towards me and tried to put his arms around me. I quickly put the light on and ran up to my room absolutely petrified of what he might do next. My heart was beating like a drum ... I put the catch on my bedroom door and placed a chair against the handle like I'd seen in old films.

The next day I went out of the house without breakfast I soon met the rest of the cast of Red Riding Hood at the Library Theatre Luton. These people seemed so confident and talked all the time about towns and cities where they had worked or, at least, been. They would say things like, "And how was Barnsley?"

"Well it was the same at Widness luv. I hear you're going to Morecambe for the summer..."

I introduced myself to the director, Dave Peters, who also played Silly Billy the comic. Dave was very professional as he directed the pantomime from the script but each time it was Silly Billy's time to speak he just said, "Own business."

The other comics in the show were Jackson and Collins (Syd and Dick); Kay Coleman played Red Riding Hood and the Philip Bernard Dancers. One of the dancers was a girl named Sally who I fell head over heels with instantly. As the rehearsals progressed that day the comics would say things like, "OK, we'll put the Ghost gag there – get the Wolf to do the run around here." They then went on to say, "Yyes the kitchen scene will be better here then we can do the Echo gag later on."

What was all this jargon? I had never heard any of this. We had a break and as we sat in the cafe, I mentioned about the man at the boarding house to some of the cast. To my horror everyone laughed it off and Syd Jackson piped in and said, "Well you are a lovely looking boy darling."

'Oh no,' I thought, this man called me "darling"! Maybe I should not have left ALCA. I got talking to the lady choreographer, Jean, who said, "We must look out for some different digs for you darling I know what it's like when they have the hots for you – they never stop." The next day I was offered digs with a family of one of the cafe ladies... a lot cheaper and peace of mind.

The start times of the rehearsals or call times got earlier and some nights we stayed till 10.00 or 11.00 at night. I remember one tea time Aubrey Philips the executive director came down to Luton after directing a few other pantomimes I think he had quite a few at the time including some very big dates. He watched me go through my script as the Wolf and said, "Stop! Stop! Stop! Right there! If you carry on like that you will have no bloody voice left!"

Aubrey was holding a plastic beaker in his hand as he spoke and then beckoned me to the front of the stage. As I got close to him I could smell it was neat rum in the plastic cup. "Steve ... let me show you how to do it," said Aubrey. He picked up the book and bellowed like a Shakspearian actor "I am the demon wolf and I have come to seek Red Riding Hood!" After that he continued, "You see darling (there's that luvvy word again) Steve, it's from the chest not the throat as you are doing. Try it."

I did try it and said in my deepest voice, "I am the demon Wolf and I have come to seek Red Riding Hood, she is just the kind of morsel I would like for my Christmas Dinner." Aubrey clapped his hands, smiled and said, "Well done young man! You'll go a long way because you listen! Did you hear that cast, this boy listens!"

The wages were more than double what I earned as an apprentice but I soon found out it was hard to survive on the showbiz road. Pay day was Friday and I remember one Thursday having to decide wheather to eat or buy a pint of lager which would get me to sleep (in those days one pint was enough). The next day, mad hungry, I awoke to do the matinee. I was doing the Run Around, being chased around the theatre as the Wolf by Dave Peters who was playing comic. When I got to the back stalls Aubrey was hiding behind the thick velvet curtains, he put his hand through the curtain and gave me a brown cash envelope and said. There's your money – and you're not worth that. Soon Dave Peters was closing the gap between us and apparently Aubrey did the same to him. When we had finished the scene we all fell about laughing at Aubrey's antics.

Aubrey's stable of acts consisted of a few old timers like Bryan Johnson (Take Me High High High), Charles (Carry On) Hawtrey, Danny Ross and some other great supporting pros. I don't think any of his artistes were on big money and some of them never had been or would be, but there was a great sense of cameraderie between us.

We travelled on to Oakengates to present the panto there and most of us stayed in the same hotel. One night we all had 'drinks at the bar' and afterwards went up to our rooms, shall we say – rather jolly from the experience. The next morning I woke to find all my money had gone!!! I went downstairs to breakfast and the company manager John Southerhurst took me to one side. John said, "I found your money on the stairs and here it is, you're a very lucky, young man." He was right, I was and I was very grateful as well as noting an important lesson – never neglect your money!

Back to normality and after that never-to-be-forgotten summer of 1972 it was time for me start work as an apprentice at George Sumner Ltd. I don't really know how I was feeling at the time but I think my head was into my new apprenticeship but my heart was back there in Blackpool listening to laughter and applause.

All the apprentices had to "off the job training" during their first year so I found myself at Bardsley Training School with one day off each week for "day release training" at Oldham College. This included night school which was, of course, wonderful for me. I could not get enough schooling – I don't think!

At Bardsley we were trained to use milling machines, lathes, welding equipment and even a spell in the electrtical department. Most of my time was spent dreaming of a career in show business but I must admit that it did occur to me to learn while I had the chance as it might help with prop making and other aspects of theatre and shows. Even today I still use many of those skills for making props and also for creating Dames' head-dresses and getting them perfectly balanced. There is always a danger that they might fall off during a performance but the teaching I had then has held me in good stead to this day.

While I was making progress as an apprentivce engineer I was also getting a few gigs from agents like Madam Ace, Johnny Smart, JT Promotions, Dave Lee and also a few from my friend Mike Constantia.

I also met at Bardsley Training School a man by the name of Jack Shenton. He was indeed the boss of the school and was also very busy with youth club organisations. He was a freemason too sohe was well connected. Every day at break time Jack would snark his lip like Humphrey Bogart and say: "Right lads, breaks over."

I couldn't help myself, I just had to impersonate him and, of course, the inevitable happened and he caught me in the act. He told me to go to his office. Everyone thought I was for the high jump, me included, so imagine how I felt when he said: "Why don't you do it? Come to my office with me."

Everyone thought I was in real trouble – me included. He didn't say another word but briskly led the way to his office, ushered me in, motioned for me to sit down and then closed the door before sitting down himself.

"Instead of messing about impersonating me, why don't you come to one of my youth clubs at Royton and organise a show," he said.

I was totally surprised. I had been steeling myself for a real telling off but instead he made me an offer I certainly couldn't and wouldn't refuse. Did I do the show? You bet!

I went to Jack's youth club and we did indeed do a show and that was followed by oldham Carnival in which I dressed as Ken Dodd – my hero – and had a string of Diddymen behind me all rattling charity tins.

I think it was a double ploy on Jack's part because he got something else going on at the youth club but also finally engaged me with young people of my own age. It worked because I made many friends at Royton Youth Club and still value them.

At Bardsley I lasted a whole year but was really dreading having to actually go to work at George Sumners Ltd. It wasn't their fault, it was just the way I felt about things. So, I started looking at job adverts and saw an ad in the Oldham Chronicle for an apprentice development engineer at ALCA Electronics, company owned by Alan Carter who was rumoured to be a Chicago gangster though I think that some people might have been getting mixed up with ALCApone!

I phoned them and got a job interview with a gentleman named Earl Fisher who was the managing director. I didn't know what to expect because of the rumours but it was an easy interview and I got the job which turned out to be brilliant as I had to combine engineering and electronics, my mentor being Stan Alston who was a really great guy.

One of Stan's tips was, "Wherever you go, make sure you have a screwdriver in your hand, then it looks as if you are in the middle of a job even if you are just having a chat about football."

The job was Development Engineer was one that many of the blokes wanted because they had to do piece work while our main role was to think up new ideas for amusement machines. I had reached the promise land as far as prop making was concerned. I was able to walk into any dept. and ask the foreman to make whatever I wanted, always making out it was for the job in hand, of course.

During that time I entered a talent show at the Railway Hotel, Royton. It was a special promotion being jointly run by Butlins and the People newspaper. The prize was a week's holiday at Butlins and I thought I might as well give it a go. In part it was another chance to get in front of an audience. As it turned out I won the heat and then the final and won a week at Barry Island where I was expected to take part in the talent show there as well.

I must say I had a great week. I was a lad on holiday by myself so I could do whatever I wanted. I met a few people like Mike Onions who was a Redcoat at Butlins for quite a few years and a really top entertainer. I also met Arthur Tolcher who was an actor and a brilliant harmonica player. He became famous for his many appearances on the Morecambe and Wise television shows. There were others like Lew Williams, Roger Dean and Reg Dixon who was a great comic and had his own show. He was not Reginald Dixon the famous Blackpool organist but he did come from Blackpool and really knew how to hold an audience and put on a show. The Reg Dixon show was promoted by another great name of entertainment, Bunny Barron, well-known as an impresario.

During days off from the talent competition I would watch the Reg Dixon Show and I remember him doing a great routine to Three Wheels on My Wagon. One day I walked up the steps towards Reg's dressing room in the Gaiety Theatre at Butlins. The man himself was there and looked very tired as he threw his toupee on the dressing table just as I walked ino the dressing room I cheerily greeted him and said, "Hello Mr Dixon, I'm Steve Hutch and I want to be a comic".

Reg looked up at me as he touched up his make up and said with a sigh, "Oh Son. why do you want to suffer!"

I won a further week's holiday and then a place in the final heats which were to be held at Clacton. The performers there were very different and not the the friendly bunch at Barry Island. I think there was much more at stake and a lot more tension. The prize was £1000 and an appearance at the London Palladium. More at stake indeed.

Well, I made it to the final but that was it, I came away empty-handed but as my Dad pointed out, it had been a great experience and I had met a few new people, learned a few things and realised that I was well and truly bitten by the incurable disease of show business.

I would have been happy working on the amusement machines at ALCA were it not for the Butlins experience and I knew I had to try and get more professional work as an entertainer. It was a good time for someone like me because there were still many clubs and theatres about which wanted the kind of act I could offer. It is much more limited now but I was able to increase my club work then.

I used to get bookings at places like Blighty's in Farnworth, Bailey's at Oldham and a few nights at Jester's in Mexborough.

I would take almost any booking just to be out there performing and learning my trade. I even took the dreaded three-spotter clubs. What are they? You may well ask.

In somewhere like Manchester where the clubs were fairly close together you could do a spot in one club and then go to another and do a further spot, sometimes even a third one at yet another club. That was at places like Talk of the North, Dolce Vita and others. That was hard work but good because you had three different places and three difrrent audiences.

However there were other places where they wanted you to do three spots in one night at the same venue in front of the same audience, some of whom would get progressively more drunk and thus more difficult. To add to the fun, somehow your third spot was often to involve getting the audience to dance which was a little difficult when you were basically a comedian.

I learned the hard way that in these venues if I did a kind of twenty five minutes warm up spot which gave me a chance to weigh up the crowd for the next spot then I could do around 35 mins to 45mins main comedy spot. Hopefully they laughed so much that there was only time for a ten minute final spot in which I sang a bit, did a couple of gags and got them on the floor. It was not my strongest spot but it usually worked and one night I came off and slumped into my dressing room chair and I realised that I actually had my own one-man show!

That gave me more confidence and I even extended the final spot with some ad-lib comedy and everyone was happy including me with my own show. During this time as well I was offered the chance to play the Wolf in Red Riding Hood panto. I couldn't resist it. I threw up my job at ALCA and devoted myself to the six-week panto which then went on tour for five weeks. I waited for other offers to come in and indeed one did – a return to my job at ALCA!

Yes, I took it and completed my apprenticeship.

In 1975 I decided to take the plunge and type a letter to the Trevor George Agency in Torquay. It was miles away from Oldham of course but they had a good reputation. I was thrilled to get a quick reply and a chance to audition for them at a club in Torquay.

I travelled down by coach and it seemed like I was going to the other side of the planet. When I got there Trevor and his wife Billie (Isabel) greeted me like an old friend and I discovered I was to do a twenty-minute spot during the middle of the evening.

I was keen to prove myself and actually did 45 minutes. The next day when we were discussing it Billie gently but firmly told me, "Here in Torquay we only do 20 minutes – so there is work to be done young man."

My face fell but soon lifted when they told me they would like to book me for Christmas and the following summer of 1976 plus a sole management deal. I was so excited that the long coach journey back seemed to take even longer. Trevor had treated me like a father and Billie had been very caring and I could not wait to get back there for the Christmas show.

Within a day or two I had received written confirmation of everything they had said and a request to go a little earlier for the Christmas show so that they could go through the act with me. Trevor was very good to me and kindly took apart my act and put it together again in a way that would make it work better and be more professional. They drummed into me to take good care of my props and to choreograph my act properly so that it was smooth. Audiences prefer their entertainers to know what they are doing rather than look as if they are making it up as they go along.

It's 1975, it's nearly Christmas and I'm with Billie and Trevor George and all their lovely family staying at 42, Marldon Road, Shiphay, Torquay. I stayed with Billie and Trevor quite a lot that year so they could keep a close management eye on me.

Billie, Trevor's wife, took me under her wing as she had with a young Michael Barrymore a few years earlier. Billie was a very busy lady starting early mornings with the Agency work then later taking me into their front room to tweak my act as known. 'Act As Known' is an old theatre term seldom used nowadays; I must confess I had no AAK at the time. I was working northern clubs where you had to stay on your metal and I got used to changing my AAK as I went along! This skill as helped me in my proper showbiz career as I can read a room straight away. However this was not what Billie and Trevor wanted for their string of Cabaret dates in Torquay and beyond. I was surprised when they gave me cabaret contracts requiring only a twenty minute spot. Even then in clubs I would do at least forty five plus false tabs. So we are in the front room of Billie and Trevor George. Billy sets up the front room as a cabaret floor with an Uwebank to the centre as a microphone stand and a waste bin to stage right.

"OK," Billie says, "You're announced ... what do you do first?"

I say, 'Walk on and wave at the audience'. Billie says, "No no no dear. You walk on smiling all the time with your head up, back straight and smile again at the audience whilst you pick the microphone out of the stand with absolute confidence! You then start your opening song ... Then you go through your routine of impressions at the same time working to all the room like in a circus ring, but you do not throw the props on the floor."

Billie went on, "Everything has a place. When you have finished with the Ken Dodd wig and tickling stick you place it in the waste bin to your right!" So basically Billie George taught me my AAK, telling me that you must learn your AAK word for word, then if you're in trouble on the Cabaret floor you will not fluff or stumble. He also took the time to show me how to link what I said to the next gag or impression. In other words taught me the greatest thing comics do ... have a reason for doing a particular gag or impression.

For instance, 'This man goes into the doctors with a Frog growing from his head, the doctor said how long have you had that then? The frog says I don't know it started as a boil on my bum! (Seamless link here) Then he came out of the doctors and saw this fellow ... etc. etc. into next gag.

I will never ever forget this wonderful lady for how she helped me earn my show business living. After a few more sessions like this Billy and Trevor invited me to watch their own mind reading act at Churchill's Night Club Exeter. It turned out to be a night I will never forget as long as I live. I watched these two brilliant pros take to the stage. They were absolutely 'word perfect' and it paid dividends. The night before I had had a 'bad night' in Plymouth to a party of sailors on leave, which if I'm honest just destroyed my attempts to entertain. I ended up stuttering and spluttering my act. This was obviously on my mind whilst I watched Billie and Trevor's cabaret and, at the same time, drowning my sorrows with 'Rum and black'. It was not the right thing to do when at 19 years of age all I had ever drank was two halves of lager and a packet of crisps. Needless to say I was very ill in Trevor's car on the way home to Torquay!

Trevor always called me Rufus as I had red hair in those days, and a client he traded with had the unfortunate name of Johncock. So Trevor would joke you need a new stage name what about Rufus Johncock? Trevor and I always had a good repose we would always do the same cross over gag at dinner or where ever. It was the Gorilla gag

TREVOR I say have you heard about Carruthers?
STEVE No what's the chap been doing?
TREVOR He's been co-habiting with a Gorilla
STEVE was it a male gorilla or a female Gorilla?
TREVOR A female Gorilla of course – after all, there's nothing kinky about Carruthers!

WE met recently over forty years later Trevor in his nineties and whilst we had dinner he remembered every line of the gag and, may I add to my own embarrassment, me being ill on the way back from Churchill's Exeter!

The Christmas shows in Torquay went OK but it was a little new to me and I don't think I had a good rapport with the audience. As a result I started to stutter again, something I had mostly left behind. My nerves began to get the better of me. I felt a bit depressed because I thought I had let myself down a bit. I went all right but not as good as I would have liked.

I was half expecting my summer season and my "sole management" to be torn up but Trevor George was as good as his word and confirmed the long summer season in Torquay. I couldn't wait.

CHAPTER SIX

Return of the Stutter!

Yes, I'll admit it, I was very excited about the summer season of 1976 but I was scared stiff too. Everytime I thought about how important it was to go really well, the butterflies in my stomach seemed more like a hive of angry bees.

The season began fairly early at the start of May. That was not unusual in those days although it is virtually unheard of now. I arrived at my flat on Daddyhole Plain, a well-known area of Torquay. I found myself next door to comedy legend Eddie Grant (no, not the one with dreadlocks) or Eddie P. Allen, as he had become known.

It was one of the hottest summers ever and it was hard getting to the venues since I could not drive at that time. One morning about 9.00 am I woke up Eddie and reminded him that we had to get out early otherwise we would be late for Billie's rehearsal.

"OK mate," he said, surprisingly cheerfully and then added, "Jump in the car."

We set off down the Torquay streets and Eddie headed the wrong way. I could feel a bit of a panic coming on as I thought of Billie waiting for us like an irate landlady with a rolling pin at the ready. "Eddie," I said, trying not to plead. "Where you are going?"

He remained cheerful and replied, "Oh let's just go in here for a livener!"

It was a bar of course and really not for me at all but it had become part of Eddie's life and I had to go along with it since he was my voluntary driver.

After a few weeks it was quite clear that my act was not going down well with the audiences. I know it might sound strange but looking back I think I was trying too hard and was too nervous about the whole. The worst thing that could have happened did. My stutter came back . Once that happened the audience gave up on me because they couldn't follow me and my timing was totally wrong. I felt awful. It is no fun when you die a death.

One night Trevor said, "Steve I need to see you in my office tomorrow morning at 9 o'clock sharp – make sure you put a shirt and tie on!"

I was not expecting good news and the night seemed to take forever as I failed to sleep. Eventually I arrived at Trevor's office and it was almost a relief when Trevor sat me down and said, "Steve it's not good, the stutter has got the better of you. I'm sorry but we're going to have to let you go."

I was expecting it but it still hurt when those words finally arrived. However, Trevor quickly went on and added, "Nevertheless, the good news is that I have found a job you might be interested in at the Torbay Chalet Hotel which is out at Paignton. You will be their new Entertainments Manager, if you want."

I'll never forget that. Billie was a rare diamond. What agent sacks you and then finds you another job straight away?

I didn't need to think about it, we discussed terms and I was on my way immediately. I was still only 20 but that didn't matter to Bob and Esmay Hooper, the directors of Torbay Chalet Hotel. They gave me a warm welcome and my confidence started to come back straight away even though it was quite a posh place and a good standard was expected in every department.

I have to say I enjoyed every minute of being there. I ran all the entertainment, hosted everything helped by children's entertainer Frankie Parker who was a great character. Frankie was an old pro of quite some years but did not actually exist as far as the authorities were concerned. He never paid tax or national insurance and always bought a car with tax on it so that he didn't have to show up on the official radar. He was a children's entertainer and good to work alongside.

Torbay Chalet Hotel was just what I needed. We did midnight

cabarets with Frankie playing the organ and I was also involved in the admin as well as running the bingo. I was busy but loved it and there were plenty of pretty girls on tap each week.

It was great fun, a great working environment and my stutter packed its bags and left. In the end 1976 was a brilliant summer season with the possibiity of a return in 1977.

It was during that long summer of heatwaves in1976 that I met Duggie Chapman. Duggie became one of the most notable old-style impressarios of traditional theatre but in those days he was a performer and producer with a decent reputation.

Duggie had been invited by Frankie Parker and I first met him while I was in full voice and mid-flight calling the bingo numbers. Duggie came alongside me and quipped, "Hope you're not pinching too much."

When I had a break we talked properly and about the possibilities for panto later that year. Duggie said he would be in touch but in truth you get used to people saying that and not meaning so while I liked Duggie I adopted a 'believe it if or when I see it stance,' he said.

After his visit the long hot summer continued and I enjoyed virtually every minute in my role as Entertainments Manager of Torbay Chalet Hotel. It sounds a bit like Fawlty Towers now but believe me, it was great.

During that summer Michael Barrymore was in his first big show for George Mitchell, the famous Black and White Minstrel show which starred Roy Hudd. Roy was a bit of a hero of mine because he was there up in lights and thoroughly deserved his success. He could sing, dance and was an excellent comedian with great timing and a lovely peronality that audiences absolutely loved.

So, being star-struck, I wrote to Roy and to my delight and surprise he invited me backstage 'for a gargle'. I still have the letter in my scrap book. It was a thrill to meet him and especially when he said, "So you like Max Miller do you? Well you'd better try his hat on!"

He actually owned one of Max Miller's hats and had it with him in the dressing room! I excitedly tried on the hat of Max Miller, another of my heroes. It was a magic moment provided for me by a great guy. I kept in touch with Roy through the years and he even mailed me a Max Miller song he used in his act years later. Now I'm proud to be his Brother Water Rat.

Also in that show were David and Pauline Conway who I would work with later and still keep in touch with.

Finally the summer season ended and I returned to Oldham. I was already booked for the fololowing season back at Torbay which was good but it was oly October and there was still the winter to get through and find some work.

Looking back now this might sound a little strange but I actually went to the labour exchange looking for something to do and spotted a job as Father Christmas. I went to the desk and was told that I was too young at twenty. Obviously the person I spoke to had never heard of make-up and costumes. Anyway I rang the store – Lewis's – myself and said I was an actor and could make it work. They asked to see me and I took along some photos of me dressed as an old man which were taken on the summer season as I'd played Charlie in Music Hall to Frankie Parker. I got the job. There is a Santa Claus after all!

While I was doing my Ho-Ho-Ho bit one day the manager came to see me looking rather serious. I thought I was in trouble for something until he told me that there was a VIP coming to the store especially to see the toy fair and that security would be very high and we were all to be on our very best behaviour. As if I would be anything else???

The VIP turned out to be another of my heroes – HRH Prince Philip, Duke of Edinburgh. I was told that I must not speak to him but just sort of be there.

On the day though I just couldn't resist it and he stood in front of me in my full Father Christmas outfit, I just blurted out, "Hello your Highness, Merry Christmas," and stuck out my hand. I waited to be shot by security but he just smiled, shook my hand and said, "Merry Christmas to you too sir."

The press photographers loved it and the only clicking was not of guns but of cameras. I still have a much-cherished copy of the photograph. I was very glad that His Royal Highness did not sit on my knee and tell me what he wanted for Christmas because he was much bigger than me!

As if life could not get any better I had a phone call from Duggie Chapman. He was true to his word and offered me pantomime at the Charter theatre in Preston with Frank Carson and Roy Barraclough.

I was to play a Chinese policeman and once I knew I went to a lot of trouble with the makeup which I felt had to be very oriental and complicated. I always believe that whatever character you are playing on stage make-up is absolutely vital. You can have a fantastic costume but if your face looks like a pale moon you will look more like a zombie than a dame or, in this case, a Chinese policeman.

On the day of rehearsals Tom Howard the director said 'Oh just put a bit of pancake on you'll be alright with that'. Great advice of course, up to a point. It is always best to 'keep it simple' but it still has to be effective. I think make up is a little misunderstood in show biz. In the old days of 'Lime lights' of course, make up was very necessary as the spot light gave a green hue to the actors. Although these days stage lighting has changed, when I do a variety date with an old pro out comes the five and nine, or its equivalent ... red dots and the lot. One entertainer confided in me that he does not feel the same without 'slapping up'.

So we rehearsed at the theatre from about ten in the morning with the MD Norman Gent at the piano. There was Tom Howard who played Abanaza as well as directing, a very young Beryl Johnson who played the princess, Paula Curtis (need to confirm name) who later married Nelson Firth Jnr, Gina Millington who was dance captain and we had an eight piece orchestra. My partner in crime as Chinese policeman was ventriloquist Chris Corbally. Roy Barraclough was Dame but right until day 5 of rehearsals there was no sign of Frank Carson. Frank was either filming The Comedians for Granada TV or doing stand-up somewhere.

As for the Chinese Policeman, I remember that Chris and I were kind of thrown together so in addition to playing policemen we also had to make up a front of cloth spot of about eight minutes. I took the script writing lead and directed a young Chris to 'come on with the doll and do what vents do!' Then He would introduce me as Eric Morecambe. I punched the tabs from behind and appeared through the tabs centre to do my routine.

What I had not reckoned on was Chris was still being on stage with the doll. He kept interrupting my gags. We ended with some chat together but his doll had a kind of false hand (which was his own hand) and kept stroking my long red hair. One matinee I lost my rag (like redheads do) and smacked the doll around the kisser. When we got back to the dressing room I told Chris quite firmly 'you do that again and after I've smacked the doll I'll smack you! I'm not proud of that but in that situation there is not much else you can do to express yourself for the good of the show.

Roy Barraclough and I got on very well. We had previously met at Yorkshire TV studios with Les Dawson. Roy came from Preston but lived in Oldham at the time, I found him a really generous man. Roy would often take a group of cast members out for supper or lunch and gave me a lift in or out of Oldham. As a performer he was electric as Twankey with quick adlibs etc. One of his more notable ones were when Abanaza beckoned Aladdin into the cave Roy quipped 'Aladdin don't take any toffees', I guess the pc brigade would have commented on that one today, but they were different days, a time when funny was simply funny and not complicated.

One Wednesday matinee Roy had a visitor. It was Les Dawson who was sat in Roy's dressing room, I couldn't wait to go in and say hello. We chatted about our last meeting when I did Junior Showtime then Roy asked Les what he thought of the pantomime. Les took a drink from his whisky and said 'Roy, Steve, I've watched this panto and it's like Emmerdale Farm in black and white'. I guess Roy was an inspiration to me wanting to play dame in pantomime as he looked as if he was having so much fun on the green. The other thing of course was that he was admired by the other cast members.

During this panto Frank Carson was, of course, just Frank and always stormed the audience (and the band). Each time he came off he would say 'Uncle Frank wins again' and did a great trimmer phone impression. I recall him always being on the phone to his agent. Every time I appear at the Charter Theatre now I can still see Frank standing by the pay phone taking down dates etc. Frank was as straight as a die, no edge to him. One day I said 'Frank how can I improve my opening spot?' Frank replied, 'Stop doing long jokes and just do one-liners, the audience have come to hear jokes not stories."

Frank was always on a diet and people gave him crates of beer which he passed on to the other cast members and the band. One day I was cutting Frank's hair and he said, 'Steve how would you like to meet Spike Milligan? He's coming to see me next Monday afternoon. We could go for a curry with him.'

The Monday came and we duly went for the curry in-between shows. Frank and Spike were signing autographs in the Indian restaurant while I looked on. We ordered the starter then when Spike was asked which main course he wanted he replied, 'I'll have the carpet please'. Even Frank was stuck for words on that one!

Whilst waiting for the summer season to start in April it seemed a long financial wait so I filled in with a proper job repairing hairdryers and toasters and other electrical appliances at PIFCO Ltd in Failsworth ,Manchester. The other lads and I were young and full of fun and really should not have been doing this sit-down job. You can guess the banter between us.

At the time there was a TV programme running called The Prisoner starring Patrick McGoohan. You may remember it in which case you will remember the huge white ball which followed him around everywhere to stop him escaping. Well, one day whilst at PIFCO I'm sat at my bench and at the top of my voice shouted 'I am not a number I am a free man'. This prompted one of my mates to shout back 'You are number six' to this one of my other mates shouted 'who is number one' just like the TV programme … I suppose you had to be there but even now I chuckle at this banter which was great for releieving the boredom and at least got a laugh which was what I was all about really. . Being able to get a proper job because of serving an apprenticeship in engineering has always been a good source of material and I think it keeps your feet on the ground a bit. Later in my life these skills were to help me to build props for my pantomime dame seasons.

Well at last the summer season

At last the summer season came and it was time to say goodbye to PIFCO and head down south back to the Torbay Chalet Hotel in Paignton. I couldn't wait even though they always say your first summer season is always the best and that's how itg turned out to be.

When I arrived at Torbay Bob and Esme Hooper, the directors, were there to give me a great welcome but I could sense Bob had something on his mind, something he had to tell me. So, I was a bit worried when I was taken to Bob's office and he dropped the bombshell. This season I was not to be entertainments manager but children's entertainer!

There was a new guy who was now going to be entertainments manager. Apparently he had worked on the ships. Fair enough I thought although I was very, very disappointed. When I met the guy – Bill Dupree – I wasn't impressed. Instead of talking about doing late night cabarets, he seemed only interested in discussing playing Frogs by the pool because that's all he knew – pool games and the suchlike. It was very unlike working with Frankie Parker who was a genuine old pro and could sing, do jokes, play the xylophone and accompany me on the organ. Now I had to sort the kids out and play number two to a smiling assassin who played Frogs!

Well, I soon got to grips with my new position. I must just say that I wouldn't want you to get me wrong. I love kids – I used to be one! I couldn't eat a whole one though – as W.C. Fields famously said. I did feel that being a kids entertainer cramped my style a fair but but it was all right for now.

The original name for the TBC kids Club was the Torbay Tigers which made them sound like a rough, tough ice hockey team. They weren't that bad though – no, honestly. Remember I was only 21 so I had to use what I had learned from panto to keep them under control and on my side.

I taught the kids a new Torbay Tigers Song which was in fact an old panto song – 'Why does a brown cow give white milk when it only eats green grass'. Yes, very useful. Whenever the kids seemed to be getting out of control out came the song.

In those far flung days there was a joke amongst pros that basically you can always tell a real pro by the way he or she reads the back of the Stage and Television Today newspaper first because that is where the jobs were. So yes, I'm on summer season and it's May but I'm still taking that trade newspaper and, of course I always read the backpages first.

On one occasion in addition to the classic adverts like Joseph Hoyles Comedy Script Writer; Ronnie Hoyles Unexpectedly Vacant, Dancers Wanted, Costumes for Sale and so on, I read. 'Wanted – Young Comedy Impressionist for long summer season Jersey CI'.

Yes as I ripped the newspaper advert out in eager anticipation and rushed to my typewriter to start my application I could feel a sense of hope in this situation. Torbay Chalet was a bit of a village really because about two days later one of the pool attendants said, "Hey Steve there's a letter for you at reception and it's from London!"

Yes indeed, it was an audition to take place in a pub at Tavistock Street London.

I must admit I sneaked a day off and travelled from Torbay to London. When I arrived there were acts of every description, magicians, singers and impressionists all doing what we called a cold audition which means you have to perform with no audience. If memory serves me correctly the guy doing the auditions was John Smith who was the manager of Fort Regent, Jersey.

He auditioned this older impressionist who was doing impressions of Al Jolson, Edward G Robinson and Co and used the old routine The Hollywood Party which went something like, 'Last night I went to a Hollywood Party and James Stewart was there he said ……' and so it went on – very contrived.

I confess I was eavesdropping on the conversation he had with John Smith. When asked how much he wanted for the week the old impressionist said, "Oh erm …… Splutter splutter…Shall we say £225.00. When it was my turn, I said, "Oh it's £185.00 no commission, plus accommodation and fares." Bingo! – Got the job. It was a proper summer season job too from June to October working for Dick Ray International.

Of course I was thrilled to bits but at the same time I was concerned about how I would break the news to my friend Bob Hooper.

As I took the train from London to Torbay that evening I kept thinking how would I tell Bob. I didn't want to let him down but I had to think of myself too. I was turning my back on Torbay Chalet? I didn't sleep much that night my head was full of 'Am I doing the right thing?' After all I had a job for life at Torbay Chalet Hotel if I wanted it.

The next morning I had breakfast and told mself to just speak to Bob straight, no excuses – that would be best. I went to Bob's office but he was out, either in the kitchens or sorting out some staff drama, there was plenty of that at Torbay Chalet. I needed to be free to travel to Jersey in two weeks' time so I really needed to speak to Bob.

As it turned out I need not have worried on that score because when I finally found him he gave me his usual warm greeting in his Devonshire twang 'alright mi lover'.

I said, "Bob I've something to say… I'm leaving for a summer season in Jersey." Bob looked down at me and simply replied, "Oh OK. When are you leaving?"

I told him I aimed to leave in two weeks. He started to walk away when he suddenly turned back and said, "Listen, come and sit on the grass with me."

The summer of 1977 wasn't as hot as 1976 so I remember the grass being damp. Bob calmly said," It's Bill isn't it? You're upset because I gave him your job aren't you? Steve I had to give him the job. You know I'm a councillor and a magistrate don't you, well sometimes things are not as black and white as they seem Steve." He gave a big sigh, put his hand on my shoulder and went on, "Sometimes its politics, sorry Steve."

Two weeks later I travelled from Torquay to Weymouth by train complete with a cabin trunk full of props and a few large suitcases. I was to catch the 12 noon ferry from Weymouth to St Helier and just made it in time. The ship was still for around an hour and one of the stewards asked are you taking lunch sir? I took lunch alright, don't forget I was a growing lad of 21 years. As the ship started to move I knew I shouldn't have taken lunch and ended up wrapped in a blanket at the front of the ship. A tip – always face front if you are sea sick. Around six in the evening we docked at St Helier and I took a taxi to the flat Dick Ray had allocated to me in Columbus Street. I was glad to have arrived and soon collapsed on the bed looking forrward to tomorrow and still wondering if I had made the right move. Was being seasick an omen? The debate in my mind gave way to snores.

I was quite exciting when I woke up the next morning. Rehearsals were scheduled at a hotel just outside St Helier. The show I was in was called Diamond Lil's Stage Show and I played the part of Billy The Kid. I wasn't married of course – I was an outlaw without any in-laws!

That day I met my lifelong friend Roy Earl for the first time. He was a madcap zany comedy magician not only on stage but off stage as well. During rehearsals Roy asked if we could have a word and then politely wanted to know which impressions I did. I reeled them off … Roy looked at me relieved then said, "Oh good we won't clash then."

When I asked if he did impressions he said, "Oh no, mine are more like cartoons." Well his cartoon transpired to be a great impression of Charlie Chaplin with a mouse.

We eventually started the season at Fort Regent which was a huge venue with a skating rink, aquarium, shops, side shows and many other attractions.

It was as if Jersey was twinkling with stars that summer. One day Des O'Connor came to the second performance. He was rehearsing his summer show at the Opera House. We all went for drinks afterwards in a small bar on the complex. There was Des, Colin Keys (his MD) our musos, some dancers and myself. At the end of the evening Des said, "Any of you guys like to come to the house for a night cap?"

We all squashed into Colin's car and headed somewhere in Jersey! We got to the house had some drinks and then Des said, "I'm a bit peckish wonder if there's any food in?" We searched the cupboards and all we could find was half a jar of Marmite. I don't think any of us were that hungry after all.

Johnny Moore, Roger Kitter and Billy Dainty were all visitors to our dressing room one day. Johnny Moore quipped, "Welcome to Fort Regent folks, the next act on is the Red Arrows!"

The season was going well and audiences loved the show. August was soon upon us and we were all shocked to hear that Elvis had died. The entire island mourned his passing.

That season was a very social one, even by showbiz standards. We all went to each other's shows. There was Lambert and Ross who did a great comedy routine and also as part of the production a sketch with a rich toff (Lambert) and poor man (Willie Ross). They had all this dialog about being rich and being poor, then the toff shuffles off with the stick he'd been holding all the time but he's blind and the poor man goes off with perfect sight. A little bit of pathos to end the sketch but it never failed to draw huge gasps of surprise from the audiences.

Ronnie Dukes and Ricky Lee, The Grumbleweeds and Billy Dainty were among the stars who appeared at Caesar's Palace on the island.

One day I had coffee with music hall comic and artiste (I'm not well) George 'I'm not well' Williams. He was at Swansons, stealing the show every night. He told me lots of stories about working with the great Shufflewick (Rex Jameson), Max Miller and Hettie King. For a young man with a passion for show business this was just spell-binding stuff to listen to and very inspiring.

That same night we caught the back end of Des O'Connor's show. Des was sensational and afterwards I chatted to him about my comedy ideas. He was very nice, gave me a few tips and also an idea for a routine with a straw hat. He said, "Look, you need to have a reason for everything you do so why not hold a straw hat and say something like 'every time I try to sing a new song, when I put the straw hat on it turns into an old song' like this..." I've done that routine ever since so sincerest thanks Des.

During that same season there were many highlights for me. I was still a young man eager to learn the trade and the real fraternity of show business came out because virtually everyone treated me as an equal and was willing to help. Talking to people like Dickie Henderson was just awesome for me. Dick Ray was the agent for many shows there. Dickie Henderson walked on stage at a Sunday Concert at the Opera House and his opening gag was ... 'Ladies and gentlemen today I flew into Jersey and was met by the agent Dick Ray. You know him, he has a name like a war weapon'.

Dick Ray also set up auditions for Opportunity Knocks which had been a huge TV show and brilliant shop window for acts for a number of years. Hughie Green came to Jersey with Len Martyn.

They stopped me half way through my audition and said, 'Do it again Son but when you do the Ken Dodd impression, do the limericks in rhythm' I did exactly that, Hughie called me 'Fearless Freddie' in the press because I never fluffed. I passed the audition and was told that they would be in touch with my appearance date. Blow me but later that year Opportunity knocks was taken off the air!

I had already written to a Manchester agent, Derek Rawden Associates who had an office in St Annes Square and, among other things, arranged Andy Williams tours in Britain. I had a reply from Derek's father, Harry Rawden. The letter read, 'I'd be pleased to represent you when you get back to Manchester give me a call'.

By October Harry Rawden was my manager. I would go to his office three times a week and he got me work like I'd never known. One day he said, "Steve, I think you need a name change. You made a mistake with Steve Hutch. You need a name like Barrymore, a name that's rich in integrity. I said, "What about Nat West?"

"Don't be stupid," Harry replied and then he glanced out of his office and saw Barclays Bank across the road. "What about Nat Barclay?" He suggested. At the time they were renovating St Anne's square and you could see the bulldozers and so on. I looked through his window, saw a JCB and said, "How about J.C.Barclay?" Harry really liked that so I became JC Barclay for a while and it worked except that when I did gigs some of the bookers would say what does JC stand for?

Whilst with Harry Rawden I worked the South Wales clubs or, as we called them, The Valleys. One big problem was that I had no transport! Today this would have been impossible but not in Harry's eyes. I set off for the first one night gig on the train to Neath where I was to appear at the Neath Metal Box Club.

I remember it so well. The club was on a hill and I had to do three spots. I did the first two spots and it went down really well but as I was setting up for the third spot the punters were leaving. I said to the concert chairman, "How do you expect me to play to just three or four people?". I'll never forget his reply – "Oh boyo don't be so sensitive, all the acts have to do three spots. You see they are going because its chapel in the morning. Don't worry, there's us and the glass collectors. We enjoy it."

I'd stayed in a B&B in Neath and next morning had no idea where I was going that night. I had a phone number of a local agent through whom Harry had booked the week so at 10.00 am I rang him from a phone box. The agent picked up the phone and I explained who I was and that I would like to know the gigs for the next few days. The agent said, "Oh now then, you will need to ring me in about an hour, OK?" Then he put the phone down. After a few coffees at the bus station I rang him back and true to his word he gave me a date sheet for the next few days. This went on during the two weeks and thank goodness I was 'picking up' as I went as otherwise I'd have had no money for trains, taxies, buses and B&Bs.

The two week stint in the valleys ended and I headed home to Manchester with the grand total of £65.00 in my pocket after my expenses on the road. Over the two weeks I earned something like £650.00. I went into Harrys office and told him of my plight. As Harry took 10%, this meant I owed him £65, Harry had a heart of steel and said, "OK just give me £60.00 – you can owe me the £5.00".

I was booked into places like the Playboy Club in Manchester, Playboy Club Portsmouth, Blightys at Farnworth Bolton, Baileys night clubsand others like those. All these were full weeks with an occasional gig before my cabaret at say 10.00 pm. The audiences were tough and you had to fight the booze and chicken-in-a-basket, typical of those 1970's night clubs.

Harry was a great hustler and just loved to do a deal. One day when I was in his offices he said "OK, show me your date sheet for next year." of course I showed it to him. Harry studied it slowly shaking his head and then simply said, "That's no good." He got straight on the phone. First of all he secured a week for me with Joan England Management to do Midlands gigs. Then he rang Tyler Management Swansea and got another week in the valleys. His last phone call was to a Scottish Agent called Andy Green who I'd worked for as Steve Hutch. Harry started his spiel ... "Hello Andy I've got JC Barclay available next February – will you take a week off me?"

"Yes," Andy said and added, "But I hope he's better than that Steve Hutch you sent me a few years ago." Harry replied, quick as a flash, "Oh yes, he's much better than him Andy. What shall we say – £800 for the week?"

After about two years Harry booked me into a club in Barrow in Furness called the 99 club. When I arrived for the week's gig the poster said, 'Steve Barclay, comedy impressionist." He had renamed me without saying anything. So that's how I became Steve Barclay!

My desire for summer seasons and panto never waved but Harry advised that there just was not enough money in it, so my next summer season or panto would be a long time off.

One morning my telephone rang. It was Harry Rawden who opened the conversation with, "Got any new gags" Then he went on to tell me that his diabetes had got worse so he would no longer be trading from his office in St Anne's Square but would now trade from an office at home. He went on to ask if I could do a benefit show for him at his Synagogue. Of course I said yes.

When the date of the gig arrived, Harry was in a wheelchair and going blind. It was so sad to see him in this way. On the night of the gig I had to wear a hat and when the rabbi laughed so did the rest of the audience! I didn't get any money but boy oh boy did they give me 'treats'. Most of the audience were market traders and when I left I had a huge bag full of chocolates, after shave and all sorts of stuff. Great and generous people. Not long after this the bookings kind of dried up as Harry became more ill.

Because the need to eat became too great I took a job at Ferranti

Computer Systems as an electronics technician although I was all the time still doing clubs and the odd theatre date. By this time Harry had become so ill he had to move into a ground floor flat in Crumsal Manchester. The last time I visited him he was an amputee in a wheel chair and totally blind. As I was leaving, Harry suddenly said, "Steve I've got a fabulous idea to get some dates for you, I'll ring you in the week. "Harry was an agent to the end, full of enthusiasm and sheer tenacity.

I did the clubs in Lancashire and Yorkshire for more than 20 years and was hailed as 'The king of the Three Spotters'. Yes I could do a gig in Wigan and still live!

One night I was going through my music in a clubland dressing room. In those days I ended the act with a swing version of When My old Wedding Ring Was New. I asked the band to play me off after the song. They did just that but played me off to Here Comes The Bride!!! I wasn't sure if being able to sing was a help or a nuisance. If the comedy was not going so well then out came the songs and besides, there was no sign of a stutter when I sang!

It was high time to do something about this stutter so my doctor mentioned that his friend who he played golf with was a psychiatrist but practiced in hypnotherapy. A private appointment was set up and before long I was sat in his office hypnotised. Over the months I practiced speaking with a metronome in perfect rhythm just like singing but slower, then upped the pace of the metronome. After many months I noticed a change and to this day it has not returned.

Now I can tell talk from stutter (quick gag for the older readers – it was a TV advert from a long time ago...you see, this bloke... oh, never mind!)

CHAPTER SEVEN

There Is Nothing Like A Dame

Little did I know or ever even think that one day I would go on stage in front of hundreds and sometimes thousands of people wearing a frock! If you have told me that when I was a little going on a TV talent show I would have died of embarrassment there and then. But show business takes you on some strange journeys and one of mine has been to appear in pantomime (dare I say, 'star' on some occasions) as the Dame. Now I am a perfectly heterosexual bloke with a family so the concept of wearing a frock was not something I readily embraced. Now, it doesn't bother me at all because I have learned what it is all about.

Perhaps this is a good time to take a look at the background (I think I can say that) of the whole concept and point of panto Dames.

Personally I blame it on the Greeks. They were big on drama and thousands of people would pack into one of their fantastic outdoor theatres to watch plays that were classics of their day. Those theatres were quite amazing because they were created to allow the voices of the players to reach the back row even though there were no microphones in those days. They were experts at acoustics and shouting "Oh no it isn't!" could travel half a mile or more.

I disgress – they can't touch you for it – the Greeks did not allow women to act on stage so all parrts were taken by women. The Romans did the same. I suppose the men dressed in female costumes although everyone seems to have worn gowns or togas in those days so I guess the female parts called for pink togas and the male parts for blue togas. Maybe they did the same with their toothbrushes – which is why Max Bygraves sang that famous song, "I'm a blue toothbrush, your'e a pink toothbrush..." Sorry, I couldn't help myself.

Where were we? Oh yes, Shakespeare wrote some brilliant lines for women but the puritanical approach of the British establishment meant that their parts had to be acted by men, usually young men, probably apprentices to the theatre group. No wonder so many of them were confused.

Of course in Twelfth Night some female characters disguise themselves as men so we had a situation in which men playing women had to play women playing men.

Moving on...that is probably nothing to do with panto Dames but at least it meant that nobody was shocked when a bloke put a frock on to make people laugh.

So, who was the first panto Dame? That is really a tough question to answer. Joseph Grimaldi is credited with being the first when he played the Baron's wife in Cinderella. That was back in 1820. His version of a panto dame was much as he would expect today. He was a theatre and circus clown and played the dame as a comedy star bloke in a frock.

He is a legend among clowns and comedy students and the circus slang word for a clown is a Joey which pays tribute to the great man every time it is uttered.

So Grimaldi was officially the first man to be a panto Dame. But was he? There are other claims. It is said that a bloke in a frock in panto goes back to 1731 when an actor played the cook in Dick Whittington and played it strictly for laughs rather than to camp it up more like a drag artiste.

In 1886 the celebrated Dan Leno played Dame Durden in Jack And The Beanstalk. Dan could do it all – patter, slapstick, comedy acting – the lot. There is little doubt that he brought the house down at the theatre in Surrey because he regularly took that annual role for a number of years until he died a little prematurely at the age of 42. In 1886 he had his wife were both in that panto and were paid £20 a week between them.

Dan went on to become went on to become the greatest Dames

of all time, his last panto appearance being as Queen Spriteley in Humpty Dumpty at the Drury Lane theatre. That was in Denever 1903. He died ten months later. It was said that he had lost his mind by the time he died but he was only 42 so could it be that he played Dame so often that he began to get confused over who he was?

Herbert Campbell was another legendary comedy star and he also played dame a number of times, especially at Dury Lane where he and Dan Leno team up for a number of years, sometimes both played Dame. Apparently their performance was second to none and it was good mostly because of their renegade attitude towards the panto script and perhaps because neither really liked being Dame. Herbert died just four months before Dan Leno.

Perhaps the most important thing about the Dame is that she is larger than life, a totally off-the-wall character. Her clothes must always be completely outrageous in cut, colour and style, and, quiote frankly, she must be ridiculous at all times.

The moment she walks on the stage the audience should be able to laugh at their very first sight of her. Wigs are a very important part of the whole look, the bigger and the more brightly coloured it is the better. It is traditional for her to change costume constantly throughout the performance. If the Dame never changes costume it is pretty poor really. I know it can be difficult at times because of timing or perhaps the need for help with some of the hats and so on but the audience has paid to see the best and I can't help feeling that a Dame that does not have more than one costume is a bit disappointing.

Perhaps even more important than what she looks like is her general manner. It has to be comedy all the way through. She must never forget that she is a clown – man in funny clothes providing entertainment for a family audience who want to have fun. There is a place for drag artistes but that is not really on the stage of a pantomime.

As part of the fun the Dame has to be naughty, expect the handsome prince to be in love with her and get exasperated when her son Aladdin does something wrong or the handsome prince finds someone rather more beautiful.

Talking about Aladdin, did you know that it is believed that the tradition of having a Widow Twankey goes back to the time when there was a very popular tea from China called Tuan Kay. Apparently that is where the very first Twankey's name came from. I suppose if she was being created now she would be called Widow Teabag. Oh yes, she would!!!

Once the Dame started to feature regularly in pantomimes, it was expected in every production. Occasionally there are two as in the case of the Ugly Sisters in Cinderella but usually the Dame is at the centre of most of the comedy, the 'slosh' routines and so on.

Slosh? That's when the custard pies start flying. It doesn't have to be custard pies, it can be a bit cake, water or even sometimes a chaos in the kitchen scene which involves a lot of plates being smashed.

The late and great Sir Norman Wisdom who starred in very many pantomimes always said that everything had to be plausible. There had to be a reason for someone getting a custard pie in the face or for them to fall over. It had to be part of a story even if it was just a tale that lasted only a few seconds. There had tobe a reason and there also to be a "it could just happen" feel about what was going on in a sketch or whatever.

He was absolutely right of course – look at Norman's films, the Laurel and Hardy films and so on and you will see that the most unlikely of comic events "could just happen" and the bucket of water that soaked Oliver Hardy was thrown as part of a chain of events that occured for a reason.

Anyway, going back to great Dames of the past, George Robey always played the Dame with every ounce of his great experience and character. George had it all – he was a comedian, a straight actor, a singer and he even got a knighthood for his work, especially his work to entertain the troops during World War 1.

He was a total pro and when it came to playing the Dame he was a brilliant clown with his own costume designs, gags and a stage presence like no other. He never took anything away from his fellow cast but also added a fantastic extra dimension to every performance.

His Dame style was almost always both ugly and funny. The best Dames are like that and kid themselves that the Prince will fall in love with them the moment they clap eyes on them. The audience know better of course and that's where the fun begins.

Harry Brayne was a Londoner who cut his teeth in music hall and went on to variety. He was another comedy star who had no problem with dressing up as a Dame and became a big box office panto star. He wasn't unique but he made people laugh – what more can you ask? His style was more of the sophisticated Dame for whom things went wrong no matter how much she tried to keep her dignity. Audiences howled and came back for more.

Douglas Byng was another great entertainer who enjoyed an incredibly long career. He did most comedy routines on stage but had a favourite act as a female impersonator. He played it for laughs although he veered towards being rather more camp than clown. Interestingly he made his debut in panto at the London Palladium in 1921, starring in Aladdin as the Grand Vizier. It was not until 1924 that he started playing Dame when he was cast as Eliza in Dick Whittington at the New theatre in Oxford. It was the beginning of a beautiful friendship between audiences and Dame Douglas Byng.

Londoner George Lacey was born in 1904 and became an actor perfectly capable of tackling anything from Shakespeare to, well, more Shakespeare. He played Dame more than 60 times in different pantomimes often with a working class character who tried to speak with a posh accent but often got it wrong.

George was really well known for starting the idea of wearing a different costume everytime he – as Dame – appeared on stage. His costumes were amazing with so many variations. One costume was even a huge frock that looked like a snooker table. What a star!

We could go on and on about famous Dames and we will a little later but even those we have mentioned so far show that the best Dames and much larger than life and are real clowns in every sense, their make-up, their costumes and their way of speaking as well as their patter. Make no mistake, it is hard work and if any of you are thinking of having a go then be prepared to put your heart and soul into it – no, your HEART and soul! That's better!

So, don't try to look like glamorous Shirley Bassey, do your best to look like a rugby player in an outrageous frock.

My first dame was at the Dearngate Theatre, Northampton starring fresh from Children's BBC Simeon Courtie and a local lad, now working for BBC Radio Wiltshire. He was supported by Freddie Garrity, Frazer Hines, the Polvien Puppets and yours truly.

I was working in summer season at Blackpool for Duggie Chapman with Danny La Rue topping the bill and I was already booked to do a pantomime as Captains Mate at the Thameside Hippodrome with that great guy, Norman Collier.

One day Duggie rang my mobile and said, "How do you fancy playing Dame?" I thought he was joking and I replied, "Do you think I'm old enough?" Duggie ignored the gag and continued, "Look all you need to do is play it like you do as Wishee Washee, Silly Billy and the others but in a frock."

"Well I said, "Yes, OK then… has Norman Collier pulled out?" I had been looking forward to working with Norman who was a comedy genius.

Duggie answered, 'No there's just a change of plans but you will have to pay commission to Frank Woodruff the agent … you need to be at Northampton for press call in three weeks' time."

I gasped – three weeks?!

You may well ask, what's the problem. Three weeks to turn up for some photos! Well, I will tell you what the problem was – for the first time in my life I had to go out and buy a frock and a few other more intimate items of ladies' wear. I couldn't even say they were for a girl friend because nobody would go out with someone wearing the sort of things I would have to buy for the comic effect.

I went to Blackpool market that day and bought a pair of ladies boots size 7 (gents size 6). So far so good and my face had only gone mildly pink. The next snag was getting the actual frock. A nice lady who Duggie used for costumes was Christine Leister the widow of Roy Leister. himself a northern pantomime Dame. I rang Christine and to me relief she said, "No problem Steve, come to see me at my house in Blackpool next Wednesday – oh and bring your bra!"

As she said those words I could almost hear the loud timp drum roll they have in a circus. BRA!!!!!!!!!! I'll have to wear a BRA (another drum roll) ......What will my Dad think about this and our Trevor, my big brother.

Next day I braved the shame of a man buying a bra by going back to Blackpool indoor Market. I arrived about 11.30 am walked around the market for a while; there were lots of stalls selling bras, knickers and such. There were frilly knickers displayed with bits of feathers on them in red and black for 'special nights' in with the Mrs. Etc. That was the last thing on my mind as Ilooked for a stall that had what might be a sympathetic seller behind it.

By about 12.00 noon I had at last spotted my target. She was a cheerful looking, plump lady with curly red hair and red cheeks (not unlike the Dame I had in my mind).

I hesitantly approached the hall, looked all around me and whispered, "Excuse me but I'm looking for a bra for my wife ..."

The lady in a very business-like manner and a fairly loud voice said "Oh right chuck, what size is she?"

Oh no. I thought. I hadn't expected that one ...

"Err," I stammered, "About the same as me really."

"Oh , I understand now luv it's for you isn't it," she replied with a knowing smile.

"Yes, "I admitted. "It's for me but it's not......"

She didn't hear my explanation because she turned to the inside of the stall and shouted to her husband in a loud Yorkshire accent, "Have we any full cup bras that will fit this young man?"

If ever I wanted the ground to swallow me up, that was there and then. My face went totally beetroot. I didn't fdare look around me but felt that every stallholder and every customer in Blackpool Indoor Market was now staring at me. Funny isn't it. When you are on stage you want everyone to stare at you and laugh but in Blackpool Indoor market that was the last thing I wanted.

She must have taken pity on me and my shining red face that resembled a patio heater as she got a move on and found a bra in no time. It cost about £7.00. She put it in a bag quickly, smiled reassuringly and said, "Don't be embarrassed luv we get a lot of

Transferians here from Funny Girls".

I discovered that Funny Girl was a local drag show and I dearly would have liked to have explain that it wasn't because I was... well, it was because I was going to be a Dame. I realised that the more I would try to explain, the worse it would become so I just paid, said my thanks and scarpered

That same day I bought a wig with a centre parting and as far as I was concerned I assumed I had got the kit! Just one problem occured to me? What was Christine going to make the costume out of?

It was a hot sunny day, unusual for Blackpool, and I must have gone to every fabric shop in the great seaside resort. I settled on eight metres of blue check fabric.

A few days passed and I was back at Christine Leister's house with bra and fabric in a very large polythene bag. She looked at the fabric and said, "Oh Steve you bought loads of fabric, there's enough here to do about three frocks".

She measured me and then said, "Where is the bra luv?"

Fighting back the horrors of Blackpool Indoor Market I showed her my bra. Can you believe I just wrote that? Me, Steve Barclay, a normal bloke showing a lady my bra! Christine said, "Well it's a bit small for a Dame, Steve but let's just get you the frock made now."

In less than a week the frock was finished, I must say it was a great creation. To complement the blue check, Christine had put large yellow trim on the frock . I was so pleased with the result.

Christine was encouraging and said, "Ok luv, try it on let's see how you look in it."

I felt a fool standing in her front room wearing this Dames frock but we got through it. I paid Christine her fee which was less than her skill was worth.

Just as I was leaving she said, "If you'll take my advice Steve, next time luv – bigger tits!"

CHAPTER EIGHT

A Dame's First Night Nerves

The weeks passed to my press call at Northampton and, of course, my first appearance as a Dame. The big day was almost upon me when I booked a Travelodge at Towcester for the Sunday night ready for the Monday morning call.

I was still in the show at Blackpool of course so after the Sunday night performance I set off straight away to the Towcester Travelodge. I was a bit knackered when I started and by the time I actually arrived I was having to shake my head to keep my eyes from staring into space. Stupid really, a short rest would have made all the difference. As it happens I made it and after signing in I went to my room for a good rest.

Little did I know that the next room was occupied by a herds of elephants! I was really ready for a good night's sleep but that was not to be. The noisy 'elephants' next door turned out to be three young women who spent the entire night talking, laughing, shouting and generally having what must have been a good time – for them! Not for me, I kept tossing and turning and putting the pillow overmy ears but just could not settle. The next morning I came out of my room at least as tired as when I had arrived.

In fairness the young ladies were not to know and as I came out they were gathering their shopping bags and stuff and one of them gave me a warm smile and what can only be described as a knowing look. I suppose it used to be called 'giving you the eye' but I don't know what it's called these days. It was like a scene from an old film. I smiled back and there was a fleeting 'Casablanca' moment that could possibly have delayed both her and my departure from the motel. The thought struck me though that if she knew what was in my case – the Dame's dress and big bloomers made by Christine Leister – she might have changd her mind. Oh well, on with the motley...

I got to the Northampton press call and dear Frank Woodruff was waiting for me. He had kindly got me a parking space right outside the Derngate Theatre. I went through the stage door and Frank ushered me to my dressing room, looking at his watch. I wasn't late but Frank liked looking at his watch. We all do that, don't we? We look at out watch and then someone asks us what the time is and we haven't a clue. We have to look at it again! What is all that about?

Anyway, in the dressing room I stared at myself in the mirror and thought – here goes. I made up quickly because my idea at that time was to do a light make up not unlike Arthur Askey; I put a pair of striped stockings on and the centre parting wig and made my Dame debut in the late summer air of the Northampton press call.

In past pantomimes the press calls normally would give me an opportunity as the comedian to meet the other cast members, in particular the ladies. I met them alright but they seem to display a total disinterest in me as a bloke, then it clicked – IT WAS THE DRESS!!!!!!! Nobody was that keen to be seen talking to a bloke in a dress. How times have changed!

The next step was getting the script. In smaller pantomimes I was a big fish in a small sea and kind of held the panto together as the comic so I was used to having a fairly free rrin. Not in this one at Northampton!

The script landed on my door mat well ahead of time but when I looked at it I found that it was not what I was used to. For instance there were no gaps to fill with 'Comic's own business here' or 'Act as known' which means 'do your own thing'. It was a crisp document with no room for manoeuvre or ad libs.

The script was written by a BBC script writer and, so I was told by Frank Woodruff, was 'sparkling'. Well I couldn't see any sparkle. Should I just tell the promoter Barry Stead my concerns? Should I speak to Frank Woodruff who was acting as my agent?

As I was trying to establish myself as a Dame I thought better of both ideas and decided to chat to my friend Roy Earl who'd been in show business for years. He agreed there was no use in 'rocking the boat'. Roy pointed out that I had not been given an 'opening spot' of my own so this would be the route forward. Roy advised me very well to insist – via Frank Woodruff as my agent – on an opening spot no less than six minutes but no more than eight minutes with no dialogue on exit which meant that it would be totally a stand-alone spot.

In some pantomimes the Dame or comic does his or her own thing then has to talk to one of the characters in the script. This kills any exit and does not round-off the spot as belonging totally to the comic.

As Roy poured his wisdom into my veins I knew he was right. The six minutes came from his many years in variety where traditionally the comic did six minutes as the 'warm up' spot. We looked at the script and indeed my first entrance as Dame Trott was in fact placed in the warm up spot, so, I thought, that's the way to approach it – as a warm up spot.

After a few phone calls I got my opening spot but I had to fight for it. In general showbiz types are very unlike people, say, in engineering. As an example, if he was asked what day it was, an engineer would mostly probably say, without hesitation. it's Wednesday or whatever. Showbiz people would say, 'Well, er, mmm, I think it's Wednesday but don't quote me on that will you?' During the negotiations for the opening spot I had a phone call from Malcolm Goddard, the director. Malcolm had directed Cilla Black, Tommy Steele, Des O'Connor and many other of the big names of show business at the London Palladium. He had a great pedigree with dance, especially ballet and productions. To this day the word 'choreographer' fills me with dread and despair. I take my wig off to them, they are very clever people and brilliant at what they do. However most of them – not all of them – have little or no appreciation for comedy as they like to have order and precise neatness with no flexibility for comedic license in their itinerary.

Anyway, Malcom telephoned me. He was really stern and quite

rude and abrupt. He said 'Hello Malcom Goddard here, I'm directing at Northampton … this opening spot of yours I don't want 'over running like you comics do … its five minutes tops' … 'See you at rehearsals. bye'.

Oh no! What now? I'd had a precious minute taken from my opening spot. I rang my friend Danny La Rue who said don't worry luv 'less is best' … Danny went on to say 'I know Malcom Goddard very well, have you written the spot yet'? I replied that I hadn't. Danny said, "Well Steve, this is my advice – write five minutes, but make it so you can shave it to four minutes… she's sure to want you to cut at the dress rehearsal." She?! Danny went further. He said, "This panto is a number one with a full orchestra in the pit … use that to your advantage".

So as the weeks went on I wrote a short bit of business with opening gags (which, as Danny advised, could be edited) plus an action song called The Panto Rap. Raps were quite a new thing in those days so for the kids it was a new kind of panto Dame Approach. I wrote it with action like 'Stand up, sit down' on every couplet and wrote a different singing gag for every chorus.

Danny had mentioned 'less is best' and it was plus I had an arrangement done by a jazz muso with Hammond organ licks in it for all parts. There was no messing about at the band call and, best of all, the lads in the orchestra loved playing it!

Roy Earl advised that if the gags in the script were weak don't worry because you supply your own frocks and you can put your own 'sight gags' on the frocks for each entrance! They take no time in the script and you're the winner every time – big laugh on your entrance then into the script. That means that everybody's happy – even Malcom Goddard Esq!

At last the first day of rehearsals came round and I was to stay with a good friend of mine, Chris Covington, at his farm house in Yardley Gobion a charming little village just outside Northampton. Rehearsal time for the Northampton pantomime was two and a half weeks, a luxury I had not encountered with other pantomimes. In those pantos the rehearsals were normally about a week with lots of the business being written on the back of a fag packet or not. Chris had helped me develop my first costumes with his skills as a puppeteer, hence the rising skirts with wizardry of wires and levers.

That Monday morning in Northampton I had parked my Ford Sierra in a multi-storey car park around the corner from the Dearngate Theatre, leaving some of my costumes in the boot. Don't know why I did this to this day but on leaving the car I picked up my padded bras from the back seat. I was just walking up the hill and I heard this Mancunian voice shout from behind me, 'Hey! Show us your tits!" It was none other than Freddie Garrity with a handful of dancers making his way to the Dearngate. I laughed his comments off but inside I squirmed as the pretty dancers giggled at his gag ... I would have to get used to this banter as I was no longer the comic but the Dame. When you are walking down the street in Northampton or anywhere else you have to remind yourself – I am pleased to say!

So, on the first day, all the cast met up of course. Freddie was Silly Billy, Frazer Hines was King Simian, Courtney was Jack, a pretty TV presenter whose name escapes me was Jill. We had two great puppeteers who animated a mouse – Topo Gigio – from the London Palladium. They did a short spot to close the first half and BBC's Otis the Aardvark – who did his lines via ini disc – a new medium from a box on set with the operator inside. The lady who operated Otis was just brilliant. With no words, just the way she controlled Otis, she was able to shoot Freddie down one night and he had no come back!

In addition to these cast members was Paul Kidd and his wife Hazel. Paul played the Giant and the back end of the pantomime cow and Hazel played the front end. Paul of course came with a tremendous traditional showbiz background in that his mother and father played Giant and Cow in all the great pantos of the past. Paul was a member of the Grand Order of Water Rats and even so early on in my career I was interested in this famous band of entertainers.

We rehearsed in a cabaret club a few minutes' walk from the theatre with painted out black rooms; I think the alternative Sean was beginning to emerge. When Malcom Goddard took rehearsals he wore smart trousers and a huge woollen scarf around his shoulders. He looked and smelled of theatre. One day Freddie Garrity, Frazier Hines and myself were rehearsing a gag which I've only done once since. It was called the 'choir gag' and involves a row of people standing in a line. They start to sing and the leader says. "Just a minute, someone's singing out of tune! You …" He points to the King or Dame or whoever and then continues, "Come with me!" He leads the person off into the wings … a gunshot is heard. The leader returns alone then starts the choir again. The same thing happens again and again until the leader eventually goes into wings and shoots himself. BLACKOUT!!

Whilst we were rehearsing, when it was my turn to make an entrance for the gag I jumped up in a cod pirouette, clicking my heels together. Everyone laughed – except Malcom Goddard. As soon as i made that entrance, Malcom shouted from the stalls, "STOP!!!!!" Then he went on, "Steve … Dame Trott, if you're going to do this ballet move, PLEASE do it correctly. You are called for 9.30 each morning when I will show you how to do a proper pirouette!!!! Next entrance!!!"

We never got it right so it was dropped from the gag. You see – Malcom was an absolute genius in dance and took it so seriously that he forget that I was supposed to be a comedy Dame!

Well, we finally opened for the first show which included press night and we were all a bit keyed up but pretending not to be. The nerves always jangle and everyone chatters away as if they were perfectly calm because they had been doing this for so long and were the perfect professional. I don't care what anyone says, n mater how long you have been doing it – if you haven't got at least some little butterfly fluttering in your stomach it is probably time to give it all up.

So there I was, making my public debut as a bloke in a frock. The things you do for show business. I checked everything before we started – knickers, bra, the lot. I had to smile because previously all I had to do was check that my flies were done up and my tie was straight.

I need not have worried because it all went really well. The stars really starred, the orchestra was excellent, the dancers dances, the effects all worked and the Dame? Well, the reviews liked me but I was just grateful that my bonnet never fell off!

The choir gag that I previously mentioned was done just before I had to sell Daisy and at one performance I'd got through my first few lines when on walked Frank Woodruff in full evening dress in stark contrast to my large check frock with the four foot high Mop cap. When I saw him I immediately went into ad lib mode. I said, "Oh look boys and girls, it's Michael Aspel. Where's your red book – they must be doing This Is My Life tonight." Not a titter!

Frank then shouted, "Evacuate the building – now!" All the theatre doors started to open and the audience started to cough and splutter...

Because we were using a gun in the previous sketch, political activists of the time had got into the theatre after the matinee and put sulphur in the guns.

Mayhem! But nobody was hurt.

After a while the audience came back in and I started the scene from the top. As the audience had already heard the jokes I put different gags into the lines, which was a lot funnier than the original script. We got a huge round of applause.

It was that night that I coughed whilst taking the make-up off and noticed bright red on my hand. Thinking it was lipstick I dismissed it ... I'd had flu for ages that season. However when I came out of the shower it happened again. I felt awful, put my overcoat on and took a taxi to Northampton General Hospital. I was admitted with a 'clot on the lung', very dangerous so I'm told.

I was off the panto for three days and when I returned I had a chair in each wing and would do each scene then sit down, something I never do in stage costumes. The good thing is that the show went on and within a week I was better although I had to have Wharfean injections (rat poison!) to thin the blood. Well its one way to becoming a Water Rat!

One thing I learned about panto at this level was that for all the personal preparation you are certainly at the mercy of script writers. My opening spot went a bomb every night and I honed it down to five powerful minutes. However once the scripted dialog started, oh man, it was downhill all the way. There's no rescue for this as the other actors are waiting for their cues so unfortunately unless you're prepared to see all the dominoes fall to the ground or keep stopping the show ,you're stuck with it. Or are you?

In conversation with Barry Stead one night he said, "I like your Dame Steve but it's not broad enough. You should have been more over the top."

So I considered this and thought – OK, so you want it over the top, do you? I went to a phone box to speak to Roy Earl who listened and said, "There's nothing else for it son, you'll have to make a sandwich." A sandwich?! "Yes," said Roy and he then explained, "Perform the script ... put your gags in ... then perform the script again." So that's what I did. Suppose the line went something like: 'Oh Jack you're such a clever little boy, fetch me that bucket of water, there's a good boy.' Instead it became 'Oh Jack you're such a clever little boy, unlike your father he thought Eartha Kit was a set of gardening tools. Fetch me that bucket of water, there's a good boy.'

Once the season had settled properly I began to relax in the part with plenty of 'sandwiches'. No one quite knew where the extra time was coming from because I still said the lines but, before my lines I'd say, 'Oh I know you're all looking at my dress, I got it from the catalogue, don't they look different when they come?... Anyway (back to the script) I've been looking for our Jack, have you seen him?' etc. All this started to work a treat so laughs came from nowhere. No one could say I'd changed the script. I also sewed big flashing eyes on my boobs and before my scripted line I'd say, 'Watch it, I've got my eye on you! Then the eyes blinked and I got on with the weak script! It seemed my frocks began to become a pipe organ full of loops and strings to operate the light gags!

One night the script writer came to see the show and in the bar afterwards he said, "I never wrote those lines you said.'

I replied, "I know, but you should have done...Mine's a large whisky and dry ginger please'.

After the panto ended I had learned about 'sight gags' and 'sandwiches' I found the sandwiches were fairly easy for me as they were just strong gags that fitted the situation. The sight gags were still something I had to fully master but then didn't I know the king of the sight gags? Of course I did. Jacko Fosset from Skegness spent his life as a clown and really that's what my Dame was all about – a clown in a frock!

CHAPTER NINE

Inspiring Dames

There have been some amazing Dames throughout the years and we have already mentioned a few of those early comic stars who found themselves pulling on a frock, usually while they had their trousers on underneath.

I would urge anyone who wants to have a go at being a clown in a frock to look at some of the performances of the last few decades as well as of some of today's specialists.

The trouble with playing a Dame is that it really is not just a simple case of putting on a wig and a costume and speaking with a higher pitched voice. That is where some go wrong and instead of presenting a loveable clown they can give kids the horrors. The bloke in the frock might think that he is being a panto Dame but to the kid in the front row he sees someone that his mother had warned him about wearing grotesque make-up and in need of a shave.

It really doesn't work like that. Even someone with a face that could win any gurning competition in the land can make for a brilliant dame if they tackle the role like Les Dawson.

Les was, of course, a brilliantly funny man with a fantastic speed of wit – try saying that after a few sherries!

Les, like most comedians and other entertainers, had his own heroes and one of them was Norman Evans and in interviews Les often paid tribute to him.

It is worth briefly looking at Les Dawson's career as it is a lesson in persistence. He did not come from a showbusiness family and lived in a small house in Collyhurst, Manchester. I know it well.

He was not a great student and couldn't wait to get out into the big wide world and see what it had to offer. One thing he knew he could do was to play the piano – quite brilliantly.

Nobody wants to engage a 14-year-old piano player though so when Les left school at that age he started working at a nearby Co-op – but not for long. He decided he could do better and became an apprentice electrician. National Service interrupted that and he served with the Queen's Bay 2nd Dragoon Guards based at Catterick in North Yorkshire.

He almost enjoyed that but did not enlist to make a career out of it. His talent for the piano led him to getting some work as a pianist in pubs. He started to get more of a feel for show business and decided to enter a talent contest at Hulme Hippodrome. As a pianist? No, this is les Dawson we are talking about. He decided to try comedy and, dressed as Quasimodo, he did his best to make the audience rock with laughter. Sadly there was no so much as a shiver, let alone an earthquake of mirth.

Disappointed, Les decided that perhaps entertainment was not for him. A few pub gigs was as far as he thought he would go so hegot a job as a vacuum cleaner salesman. Even that was not without its unusual happenings. One Christmas for instance he was out knocking on doors the day before Christmas Eve. A young woman answered the door and was clearly upset. Les decided to make his presentation and the young woman became even more upset. In the background her husband also seemed distraught.

"We've had some really bad news – we couldn't buy a vacuum cleaner from you even if we wanted to – and we could do with one," she said. "Ours has broken down."

When encouraged she explained that he huisband's wage packet had been lost sometime from he getting it and arriving home. It was all they had in the world to pay for their Christmas and it included the husband's annual bonus.

Les was devastated for them and said he would wish them and leave them in peace. He was about to leave when he thought of something that might possibly help them just a little bit and said, "Let me look at your vacuum cleaner and see if I can fix it. That might save you having to get a new one at least.". They invited him in and Les sat on the floor and took the machine apart. That was when he found the lost and still unopened pay packet and handed it to them. Needless to say those two people were very happy that they had bumped into Les Dawson.

Most people will tell you the same – lovely guy, very, very intelligent and a wit that could slice an apple in two from thirty paces.

After trying again in show busines, mostly on the Manchester club circuit he was still not really making much progress. Then he was booked to do a week at various clubs in Hull. He needed the money otherwise he might have turned down Hull which had a reputation for having tough audiences.

The first night Les died a death. The second night came round all too quickly and he was expecting it to be a disaster once again. That is probably why he had a drink or two before going on stage. Actually it was probably three or four because he walked out rather hesitantly when he was introduced, sat at the piano and suddenly realised that his hands fekt like bunches of bananas. He tried to make them work at the piano keys but all that came out was a number of notes that did not seem related.

Les closed down the lid of the piano, leaned his head on his hand and peered at the audience with a rubber-faced expression of total misery and said something along the lines of "I don't know what I am doing in this converted kipper box." He meant it but the audience laughed and the more morose he became the more they liked it.

Les Dawson had found his act and was on his way to stardom that was also helped by an appearance on the legendary Opportunity Knocks talent show. He didn't win but he convinced enough viewers that he was well worth seeing live for the offers to come pouring through.

His persistence paid off and soon he was packing theatres all over the country and starring in countless TV shows.

His venture into being a Dame came about party through panto and partly through his own TV shows in which there was always a sketch involving created "Cissie and Ada" with Les playing Ada and Roy Barraclough as Cissie. They would sit and chat about family and health issues, gossip about the neighbours and so on and all the time Les was [paying tribute to the character of "Fanny Fairbottom" created by Norman Evans.

Les took 'Ada' as the model for his panto dames. He never piled on the make-up but played himself in clown mode and dressed in the totally over-the-top costumes of a traditional dame. He was, of course, quite brilliant. He made the role his own no matter what the panto and broke box office records time after time. Whever possible he kept the name of his TV character like, for instance, in Babes in the Wood at the Manchester Palace where he played Nurse Ada.

Arthur Askey was one of the nicest people ever to walk across a stage. A great and much-loved entertainer he also proved to be a wonderful dame in panto. Arthur Askey was brilliant, especially in Charley's Aunt which is not a panto of course but is still a brilliant comedy and Arthur played dame in more than one panto just as he played Charley's Aunt.

Known as "Big Hearted Arthur" he sometimes called himself "Big Hearted Martha" when appearing in pantomimes at the great London Palladium and at all the other major venues around the country.

In an interview in the mid-1970s he once explained, "Pantomime is a great family affair and it's marvellous to hear the reaction from the kiddies… Of course, in the older days the children were enchanted by the whole thing…When I did my comedy undressing scene as dame, I used to get yells of laughter from the kids. In latter years I remove my many petticoats to the accompaniment of wolf-whistles and cries of "Get 'em off!"

Arthur was born in Liverpool in 1900. Victoria was still Queen then. He was a natural entertainer and at the age of 24 he joined a touring concert party which led two years later to him becoming one of Fred Wilton's Entertainers at the Oval, Cliftonville where he appeared for four years. In concert party with Powis Pinder's "Sunshine" in 1930 he attracted the attention of London producers, and by 1937 he co-compered "The Coronation Revue" with George Robey and that led to him being teamed with Richard "Stinker" Murdoch in Radio's "Bandwaggon". That of course, made them both household names but in particular Arthur who was a clown of the partnership.

The radio catchphrases too became household phrases – "Before your very eyes", "Have you read any good books lately?", "Hello Playmates" were imitated throughout the land, along with Doesn't it make you want to spit?" and, of course Arthur's own "Ay-thang-yew!"

Arthur went on top be a top-of-the-bill star at most major theatres and he appeared in numerous Royal variety shows. The royal family particularly liked to see his performance of the famous Bee song.

Arthur played other panto comedy roles, including brilliant performances as Buttons but his appearances as dame and especially as "Big Hearted Martha", with a minimum of make-up and not-too-outrageous costumes, that he brought the house down.

The audience wanted to see the Asrthur Askey they knew and loved and so a simple bit of greasepaint and those trademark spectacles peering out from under a bonnet were all it took to get the audience cheering as soon as he appeared on stage. Arthur Askey was one of the biggest stars of his day – and any day come to that. It was a huige loss when he died in 1982 – Big Hearted Arthur to the very end.

Another comedy star who did not seem a likely panto dame was Terry Scott but it was a mark of his talent that he was not only a dame but a really great dame.

Terry was a comedy actor throughout his career. Even when playing a very small part such as a beat copper in a Miss Marple film starring Margaret Rutherford, he had a great presence and was never overlooked. On TV, of course, he starred in Hugh and I, Terry and June and countless other shows plus Carry On films and others on the big screen. He was a great comedy actor and he could do it on stage in front of a live audience too.

His main comedy act was in playing the part of a really dreadful schoolboy but his portrayal and patter were brilliantly funny and so he was able to change from school uniform into dame's costume with confidence.

He was simply larger than life and very funny- exactly what a dame should be. He played in all the major pantomimes, knew how to fill the stage and gave confidence to everyone else on stage with him.

Terry Scott was born to be a dame.

The same could be said of John Inman of course.

John came to the fore when he starred in Are You being Served on TV but he had been around for a while before that and was a very accomplished actor and entertainer. His music hall impersonation of Frank Randle was amazing and showed that he could act, joke, sing and dance with great aplomb. Funny word that – 'aplomb'. I thought that's what posh people have in their mouths when they are speaking!

We digress. John Inman was born in Blackpool and made his first professional stage appearance aged 13. On Television he worked with Hugh Lloyd, Roy Kinnear and appeared in television's first colour musical, an oddly-named show called Titi-Puh with Harry Worth, Hattie Jaques and Richard Wattis.

John's West End debut was in the musical Ann Veronica, and appearances at the Windmill Theatre, followed by playing Lord Fancourt- Babberley in Charlie's Aunt at the Adelphi Theatre.

John went on to find fame as "Mr Humphreys" in BBC's "Are you being Served", adopting the show's catchphrase "I'm Free!" as his own, as he created one of the most outrageous characters seen on the screen. He continued to tour in farces, notably "My Fat Friend", and in Summer shows and seasons throughout the UK. The success of Are You Being Served made him an international star, with a big fan following in Australia and many other countries including the USA. He also appeared in six Royal Variety Performances.

All that and in addition John became one of the country's top pantomime dames with more than forty pantos to his credit.

It has to be said that his amazing costumes, often designed and created by him, together with his mastery of the role made him one of the finest dames to tread the boards. He specialised for a while as "Mother Goose" and appeared in that role at the Victoria Palace, and as Nurse Wanda in the London Palladium's giant panto, "Babes In The Wood".

"I like playing dame," he once explained. "It has everything going for it – fun, frills and frolics. You can't get better than that. Being larger than life on stage and having a lot of laughs is brilliant and to think that I get paid for it. Being a dame is living the dream."

Most dames share or shared that same view including the wonderful Billy Daity, possibly one of the most under-rated stars of show business.

Born in Dudley in 1927, Billy's dancing prowess was there for all to see from a very early age when he was outstanding as one of the Betty Fox Babes in Birmingham. When his family moved to London he achieved a scholarship to RADA and at the same time he became a pupil of a man called Buddy Bradley. Who? Oh, he was only choreographer to Fred and Adelle Astaire! What an education Billy had!

It was a leveller when he made his West End debut in 1942 though. He landed a panto part at the Colliseum though. He was cast as playing the back legs of the dancing donkey, "Asbestos", in Mother Goose, starring Norman Evans and Patricia Burke!

An audition for a chorus part in the George Black revue, Strike A New Note turned out better and along with his sister Betty, and the young Ernie Wise and Eric Morecambe, Billy opened at the Prince of Wales Theatre in 1943.

In 1945 Billy was called up and toured the Far East in the Stars In Battledress revue, Hello ALFSEA. After the war his first engagement back home was at the lovely little Cosy Nook Theatre in Newquay. The show was called Gaytime, something Billy never forgot because he later bought a house there and called it Gaytime.

Billy toured in Music Hall and Variety during the 1950's and topped the bill in Puss in Botts at the Pavilion, Torquay. He wasn't a dame at this stage but he was a star. His fantastic dancing and mesmerising funny walks were enjoyed by millions at theatres and watching TV, especially when he appeaqred several times on Sunday Night at the London Palladium and in Royal Variety Shows.

Billy took to playing dame like Mother Goose to water. He

not only looked the part with most outrageous costumes but his eccentric dancing and walks had audiences in stitches. To top it all he created a comedy ballet routine that was nothing short of hilarious and brought a different dimension to panto dames. He once attended a panto press reception in London in full dame costume and make-up, realised he was late for an appointment and dashed outside and onto a passing bus. I wonder if he had a purse with him?!!

Billy passed away in November 1986 but will always be remembered for his performances.

"I never thought I would play Dame," he once said. "It never occured to me and I didn't think anyone else saw me as a dame either. Then someone had a brainwave and I had even more fun in panto. You can do anything you like as a dame. You can much about, shout, sing, wear fantastic costumes and just have a great time. I loved it.

I am proud to have known and worked with both John and Billy – you don't get to meet too many legends in your own life time.

Stanley Baxter was also a brilliant dame. As I write this he is still alive but retired a long time ago after a fantastic career.

Stanley was born in Glasgow – where else with an accent like that? His father was an insurance manager and there was little hint that young Stanley would one day become one of the biggest stars Scotland has ever produced and one of the finest panto dames of all time although he was coached by his mother and appeared on stage while still quite young. During his National Service he began entertaining the troops.

Back in civvy street he cotinued to prove himself to be a great mimic and a natural clown so it was no surprise when Stanley found himself on the rungs of the showbiz ladder. He became known for his amazing impersonations which ranged from George Formby to Marlene Dietrich and even included The Queen!

He was not just a natural for stage but also for TV and radio and the Stanley Baxter show drew huge viewer ratings for many years. It was not unusual for Stanley Baxter to appear as 40 different characters in his TV specials – no wonder he reached legendary status at such an early age.

Of course, he was in demand for panto and had no problem at all in donning the frocks and starring as a dame. He often starred in both Glasgow and edinburgh pantomimes, played an ugly sster alongside such other stars as Jimmy Logan and Ronnie Corbett and with the latter, devised a comedy ballet routine among many others.

Of course, Stanley was also called upon to play Mother Goose and did so spectacularly.

Yes, Stanley Baxter deserved the Lifetime Achievement Award he was presented with at the 1998 British Comedy Awards and, if there was one, he would also deserve the Golden Frock Award for being a fantastic dame.

There have been many more great dames throughout the years, right up to today. Berwick Kaler has appeared in many stage shows and TV series but his greatest fame has come from his annual appearance as dame in York Theatre Royal's pantomime, a show which he has written and directed every year for about four decades.

He is a firm believer in traditional panto rather than relying on casting someone who nearly came third in a TV talent show as a crowd-puling star. In an interview I saw Berwick once explained: "People have been saying for years that the panto is dying. Well, some of them deserve to die. I'm talking about the ones that flout tradition by casting a young man as principal boy, or by diminishing the role of the dame, sometimes writing her out altogether. Having cast clapped-out TV stars to draw the audiences, these pseudo-pantos make no further effort. They just don't try. I dive into a tank of water every year. Who wants to do that?"

"The dame is the heart of the panto. Whether it's Mother Goose, Jack and the Beanstalk, Cinderella or Babes In The Wood, the dame is a real person, a washerwoman whose feet hurt. She must be portrayed with dignity and respect. If a false bosom is worn, it must be worn with respect. I think my dames owe more to Catherine Cookson than a cartoon character but must still be funny. I am totally against mincing or any other indication that the male dame might enjoy his feminine role too much. You mustn't make the man in the audience uncomfortable or demean women. You don't have to do any of that – just look outrageous and have genuinely funy lines and they will love you. That's what being a dame is all about – being funny, being loved and being a great asset to the show."

There have been and still are so many great dames that it is difficult to mention everyone here otherwise this book would challenge the Encyclopaedia Brittanica for size. Anyone left out, please don't be offended.

One star we cannot leave out is probably the greatest female impersonator of all time – the amazing Danny La Rue who somehow managed to be so glamorous in cabaret and in his theatre spectaculars biut could equally be such a great clown dame in panto. Danny was simply a brilliant entertainer.

Danny was born Danny Caroll on July 26th 1927 in the city of Cork but at the age of nine his family moved to London. He was smitten by showbusiness and from an early age began appearing in concert parties which then led to variety shows. Of course he did not remain Danny Carrol. He was advised to change his surname and it was suggested that he should copy a French singer of the time known as Danny Street. So Danny became Danny La Rue and didn't it suit him!

The very small Irving Theatre near Leicester Square was his first real taste of London's West End and it was mutual love at first sight. He was booked to appear at the famous Churchill's nightclub and worked alongside people like Barbara Windsor with whom he became great friends. It was actually hard not to become friends with Danny because he was so charismatic. I worked with him many, many times and it was always a joy. He was always willing to give advice and was a great team player although he was such a major star.

Continuing his story Danny opened his own club and that was hugely successful. He starred himself most of the time but other stars were queuing up to work there because it was such a great venue and a token of hoour to appear there.

As a pantomime dame he started in the 1960s, first of all as an ugly sister! Hard to imagine the glamorous female impersonator playing an ugly sister but he was brilliant of course and constantly in demand for panto year after year from producers in the provinces and, of course, in London which is why he appeared as Widow Twankey in Aladdin at the London Palladium one year.

Danny 's career flourished right to the end when he died in 2009. He played several Royal Variety shows and in all about 30 Royal shows of one sort or another. He was King Rat of the famous Water Rats, appeared in many of the Good old Days TV shows and won countless awards. His OBE meant everything to him but he was also named Entertainer of the Decade in 1979 among very many other awards.

How did he manage to bring together the glamour of his cabaret performance and the brash clowning of the panto dame. Sheer talent. As was mentioned earlier, some of today's dames tend to have abandoned the concept of the clown in a frock and have played it in a rather more camp, drag queen style. That is fine in a cabaret show but we are talking about pantomime which is just a bundle of family fun.

Danny never failed to remember that he was there to make the kids and the mums and dads laugh and he did so without forsaking who he was. He was larger than life and certainly a fantastic panto dame.

So many wonderful dames – past and present. We have mentioned the brilliant Arthur Askey and there are very many others including the excellent Jack Tripp – the entertainer's entertainer, George Lacey and even Bobby Crush who has proved that there is a lot more to him than being a great pianist.

All of these could or did give advice when they were alive and those who are still with us are very generous in their encouragement to others. If I could give any advice myself to an aspiring panto dame, it is simply to try and track down the performances of some of these great dames, study how they do it, take hold of some good bits, adapt them to your own style and always remember that you are there to make people laugh not to impress them. Be a clown – a clown in a frock.

CHAPTER TEN

How To Become A Dame

For me the best way to become a dame is to firstly become a comic which means you get to play all the comic parts in pantomime like Wishy Washee, Silly Billy, Idle Jack, Buttons and so on. Did you notice how Buttons comes last on my list?

Let me explain. It is a rare person who can take his first part ever in pantomime and play the dame. You need confidence and you need experience. Yes, it is true, you can get by and kid people will tell you how good you were. But, trust me, if you analyse yourself in all honesty you will know that it was more difficult than you thought and you could have done better.

It's a fact. I applaud anyone who is willing to try and play dame and I wish them every success but be a realist. It is a specialist job and you need to serve an apprenticeship in other roles before you go for the outrageous frock, two-ton wig and cushion-padded bra!

Some people might not like what I am about to say but I must stress that we are talking here about pantomime dames, family entertainers who can make people laugh by their dress, their expressions, their gags and their routines.

Let's look at the "Ugly sisters' in Cinderella. There has been a trend towards the "sisters" being played by two screaming Queens out to prove that they are funnier than anyone else but doing so in a rather more 'adult style' more suited to the pub or club than the panto stage. Often a rivalry springs up with the 'sisters' trying to outdo whatever other comedy character there might be.

Buttons is not an out-and-out comedy character. He is totally a nice guy who loves Cinderella but the audience knows that he will never getthe girl so they sort of feel sorry for him. He can make them laugh but there is always that air of pathos about him. When you play Buttons you are slightly restricted.

My favourite comic part has always been idle jack because he is just a clown and can do all sorts of things from slapstick to stupidity, comedy dance routines and playground jokes. He is a great, unrestricted character to play. That said, I have seen Billy Pearce play buttons and be genuinely funny all the way through the show.

Generally speaking Cinderella is the most popular of all pantomimes for all sorts of reasons – the costumes, the coach, the fairy Godmother and the feelgood factor at the end when the good guys win. It's lovely but it can be spoiled for humour if the Ugly Sisters are more like drag queens being nasty than two clowns making fools of themselves.

This in part is why I say it is a good idea to play the comedy roles first before attemtping to be the dame. That way you get the chance to watch and learn against a seasoned Dame which means that when you get to be the dame yourself, it is a natural progression!

Also if you have played the comic parts when you play the dame you know what the comic wants from you as a performer. For me becoming a dame starts from the feet ... and then up through the shoulders down to the hands with the head nodding knowingly!

When I play Dame against a comic I let him do all the walking around and so on and tend to stay static so there is no danger of pulling the audience's focus to myself while the comedy character is getting his best laughs.

Yes, you are right – I am such a kind dame! That's because I've been there myself. The comic should by all means poke fun at the dame but never degrade the dame as I've seen a few times. I've seen supposed comedy characters rip the dame's wig off or cover the dame in slosh. That's not the right thing to do. The audience really don't want that. They don't want to see the dame's wig removed – they want the dame to remain in character. If anyone thinks it's funny to cover the dame in slosh they should try cleaning the costume in tijme for the second performance of the day! Basically that sort of behaviour is very unprofessional and adds nothing to the show. It actually takes something away from it.

I believe in preparing for the part of dame properly. Once the contract has been signed I am mentally preparing for it even if the show is a few months away from even starting rehearsals.

I must confess that I have often been standing in a queue somewhere totally oblivious to the rest of the world when I have suddenly realised that some people are staring at me. I don't blame them because I then realise that I am thinking about playing the dame in a forthcoming panto and as I think about it I start getting into character – hands clasped in front of me, elbows stuck out and even my lips pursed. It must look a bit weird so if people stare it's my own fault. Needless to say I quickly change my stance and smile a little so that people known I am safe – and, dare I say, normal.

Nevertheless, mental preparation cannot start too soon only it is better when you are in the safety of your own home or dressing room at another show. I remember being in a lift once having a quick practice and I was so into what I was doing that i didn't even notice that the lift doors had opened and there I was standing funny and even breaking intothe dame's voice. There were quite a few people waiting to get into the lift. Most of them looked at me as if I was a complete lunatic but I think there were a couple of them who wanted to ask me out for a date! Of course, I'd have to ask the wife first!!!

When I think about it, I believe that my favourite dame is Widow Twankey from Aladdin. She is pretty grotesque in a funny sort of way and responds way to compliments from the villainous Abanazer who is simply trying to get the magic lamp all to himself.

The wonderful Widow needs a lot more than just the costumes and wigs, she is a really great character in her own right and gets to work scenes with just about everyone else in the cast.

Sometimes in bigger panto productions you are given a dresser which is great. Sometimes there are quick costume changes and someone on hand to help you pull one frock over your head while stepping into the next one is brilliantly helpful tto you and makes the panto run so mucyh more smooth. No excuse for delayed entrances!

My first tip if you are playing dame is to make sure you have a really close shave just before you put on the greasepaint. The reason for this is that it will go on better at the start and if you are doing a matinee and an evening performance the last thing you need is to have to take off the make-up between shows so that you can have a further shave and then put it all back on again. So don't shave when you get up in the morning, leave it as late as you can so that it will last the rest of your working day – but don't be late for the performance!

With that in mind, it is worth remembering that you will probably not be able to go out between performances because of your make-up. You should never be seen by the audience who have just watched the show or the audience coming in unless you are completely in 'civvies'. To be seen in part of your costume or make-up ruins the illusion and can spoil the show for those who see you. In short, it is very unprofessional and no artiste worth his salt would do it.

So if you need to go out and get something to eat either remove the whole outfit and make-up or stay in costume and take your chances at the local supermarket as if you are doing a publicity stunt. Better still, think head and get what you need on your way to the theatre and be prepared to just stay in the dressing room between shows. I always have a good book with me – I could recommend this one!

Unless you are only doing a one-day show it is a good idea to make your dressing room your second home. Treat yourself to a few biscuits or whatever you might have on hand at home. It will help you to feel relaxed as well as being very practical considering what we have just been talking about. Whle the rest of the cast go out to tea between performances you are kitted out with what you need and simply put your feet up and take it easy.

I remember that time I made my panto debut as the wolf in Red Riding Hood at Luton Library. I was 16 and I knew precious little about the running of a panto even though I had been entertaining for a few years. In those days we would often do three performances in a day, a nightmare for a dame who was ill-prepared but perfectly fine if the dame had got himself well organised.

So, think about your character well in advance, get your dressing room well organised for comfort and remember that you are not supposed to be trying to be a glamorous character. That is the joke of the dame being played by a bloke and it has been since the very early days of panto. Keep reminding yourself that "I'm a bloke in a frock." That way you will not be tempted to try to be anything else. If a drag queen tries to be glamorous it is totally different to a clowning bloke trying to mimic how a woman might make herself glamorous just for laughs.

The transformation really starts when you get the script. You learn the lines and think of how you are going to use your voice to deliver those lines for the best results. All the time you remind yourself that you are playing totally for laughs and if you tilt your head as you say this line or that will it get a better laugh.

When you are on stage you exaggerate almost everything so that everyone gets a clear view of what you are doing. A very slight nod of the head won't be seen. If you nod it too much it looks ridiculous and as if you are doing an audition to be one of those nodding dogs some people put on the backshelf of their car. So you have to get it just right and that takes a lot of consideration and practice, usually in front of the mirror.

Always remember that the script tells the story and gives you something to work with but to make it really come alive and irresistible to the audience, the responsibility is yours.

You need to practice all your movements – personally I find it better to start with the feet and work my way up. If I am facing an audience and talking to them on my own should I occasionally go up on tiptoe to emphasis something the dame is feeling – perhaps coy embarrassment if she is talking about being in love with someone.

If the dame is moving about on the stage will she walk quickly, slowly, saunter, cuff her feet or shuffle them – all these movements send out messages to the audience. That is why if you see any old clips of Norman Evans he used to occasionally hoist up his bust as if he is trying to be more comfortable. Les Dawson did the same. One little movement like that can have an audience in stitches if you get it right. You don't even have to say anything at that point although a hitch of the bust, a wince on the face and a quick "These wonderbras aren't what they used to be" should work a treat.

Of course it is very important to make sure you have enough time for practice while in full costume. You might have everything worked out but if you suddenly find that the little skip around in a circle on the stage that you planned actually dislodges your wig and giant hat, you have a problem and you need time to make some adjustments.

So, let's look at the make-up, After that shave apply some cream – I use Nivea. It will help your skin relax and provide a decent base for what follows. I always apply the 'pancake' with a little sponge. Remember that you are going to be under theatre lights and you need to be seen clearly from every part of the theatre. Be bold. If your face looks like an orange when you peer in the mirror don't worry about it. You may have to dance a Tango! Sorry, i couldn't resist that one.

How you see yourself in the mirror is not exactly how the audience will see you so if you are not confident ask someone to take a look at you on stage under the lights before the audience arrives. When you get used to putting on make-up like this you will do it in no time at all but give yourself time when you are starting out and then you will not have a panic on your hands when you hear a strange voice say "Fve minutes ladies and gentlemen, five minutes."

I also use a stick of eyebrow soap to smooth down my eyebrows. That is necessary because you will then use a 'pencil' to accentuate your eyebrows and other parts of your face to make you look permanently surprised. Trust me, it looks funny to the audience.

Every dame has their own style of make-up so you will have to experiment a bit. Cowjns are the same of course – they pick a make-up which is unique to them. Dames don't go that far but you have to pick a style that you are comfortable with and will also make you look funny to an audience.

I usually create arcs above my eyes a bit like you see on clown faces then I use a bright blue to fill in those arcs. Then comes a touch of red for the nose, red apple cheeks, and a couple of red spots either side of the nose which helps to bring out the brightness of the eyes.

A word about the nose – don't overdo the red. You don't want to look like a red-nosed clown or an aged alcoholic. Enough red to highlight your nose is just fine. Too much will make it sem as if you have just had a punch on the nose!

"The best slaps are the quick slaps. Slap? Well, that's what we call the make-up. Most of you probably already know that but just in case. The secret is not to overwork it. I've got the whole thing down to about half an hour on a good day.

I must at this stage pay tribute to my wife, Tracey. She has taught me a lot about make-up application and about make-up hygiene, especially around the eyes. Eye pencils for instance can become infected and the last thing you need is swollen and watering eyes.

She also taught me the important of moisturising, especially when you remove the make-up or before you go to sleep at night.

Don't ever be afraid to ask someone else about it, even if it is someone working on make-up in a shape. They will be delighted to help. As I said, my wife has been much more than helpful – it cannot be easy for a lady to teach her husband how to put on his make-up!

Now let us look at the costumes. Some pantos supply the costumes but most dames prefer to provide their own and that means either finding a costumier or at least someone who is good with making dresses or teach yourself how to cut cloth and sew it together.

You need to be mentally creative too. Design your costume to fit the panto and how you want your dame to be perceived. Is she going to be a down-trodden, penniless widow who still makes people laugh or is she going to be a larger-than-life show-off of a dame? You need to think about that and design your costumes accordingly. Yes, I did say 'costumes' because you won't want to be wearing the same outfit all the time. You would not wear the same costume when you are trying to milk the pantomime cow as you would if you are going to the spectacular wedding at the end of the show.

The costumes I usually use are my own, and I am quite proud of them. I design them myself and make them myself just as I do my other props. I have a particulare favourite, the one in which I usually make my first appearance. The costume helps establish your character so it is very important. I made most of it but I must admit that the bobbles on it were hand sewn by Tracy.

Before the frock goes on the stripey tights must go on. They are mostly invisible to the audience but I know they are there and if there was an acccidental tumble it would look like part of the gag. I have a pair of very bright, dare I say 'gaudy' winkle-picker shoes. You can put a slight heel on them to make them look slightly like a woman's shoe but don't try to wear real high heels because you will probably break your ankle or at the very least you will cripple yourself by the end of the run. How women wear them I have no idea.

I also have vast bloomers and a float-out skirt with a stupendous bra to create the buxom look essential for the dame. On top of all that I have a collection of outrageous wigs which I make myself.

I try to make as much myself as possible. I have written my own 'Dame Song' and my props vary from just little gags to an exploding washing machine. Not everyone goes to those lengths but I personally find it more satisfying.

Pantomime is often our children's initiation into live theatre. That's why we owe it to them to give it our all, and keep the magic alive. The dressing room gets you in the mood. You can see the lights around the mirrors, you can hear the audience babble through the monitors. That's when you get that tingle. You need to feel that tingle every performance. Perhaps the last thing you should do before you leave the dressing room is to just remind yourself that you are going out there to be the children's favourite aunt, someone who is loveable and makes them laugh. Win the kids and you will win the parents and they will all go home happy.

One last look in the mirror and it's show time!

There is an unwritten code for Dames. We have touched on this but it cannot be stressed enough that the Dame is someone very special, someone who canmake or break the show. So, what is the real secret of being a panto Dame? Good question. There are certain rules that are always worth keeping in mind –

By all means go over the top with frocks and other items of costume and especially hats. Your hats can be as big and bold as you like. They can be teapots, bowls of fruit, a television, a cupcake, anything you like. I have one with a tray on top and on the tree is a teaport, sugar bowls, two cups and saucers and even a spoon. It is big and very, very colourful – you cannot miss it. The kids love it. Maybe they later wonder why there was a man dressed as a woman with a tea tray on his (or her) head but at the moment of impact they love it and laugh aloud which is what you are there for.

If the Dame is being played by a well-known star the audience want to be aqble to instantly recognise him so his make-up and costumes should be outrageous without disguising him.

If the Dame is not played by someone famous then just go for it, be funny and give the audience a good time. You soon will be famous.

There are a number of other tips worth considering. First of all make sure you are thorough in your preparations. Get the script as soon as possible and go through it timer and time again so that you do not just get the words in your head but the actions too. How is the Dame going to walk? How is she going to use her hands – will she fold her arms? Will she put her hands on her hips? If there is a chase around the stage will she have a comedy run? Will she waddle?

What is her voice going to be like? Is she going to be matronly or is she going to be like a 70-year-old going on fifteen with her eyelids fluttering at the drop of her handkerchief? Remember we are talking about a pantomime Dame here not a cabaret Drag Queen.

So, prepare well in advance, also remembering that the director is the boss and may want something different to your own thoughts and ideas. Don't make the mistake of going prima donna and insisting that you are right. Try it his or her way, you might find that it is better than your own idea and if it isn't, make a gentle suggestion or two. A cast at war rarely succeeds in making for a memorable pantomime. It has to be a team effort.

What other preparations? Well, the location of your dressing room is very important. I can think of at least one venue where I have appeared and been given a dressingroom on the third floor. Can you imagine what it was like running down the stairs wearing massive frocks, a gigantic hat and multi-coloured clogs on your feet.

The thought that the Dame cannot appear in the finale because he is on her way to A & E still in full costume doesn't bear thinking about – but it has happened! Imagine the fun the hospital staff had while the Dame was trying not to swear because of the pain from his broken ankle. Imagine how he had to get his black and yellow vividly striped tights off so that his ankle could be sorted! And we haven't even got as far as the bloomers.

So, if you are given a dressing room up in the attic, work out how long it will take you to get from room to side stage and take a lgood look at the potential hazards. Better-still, see if you can atleast get a quick-change space in the wings or – best of all – ask for a change of dressing room. If you are in Cinderella you might find yourself sharing with the ponies but it would be a small price to pay.

Some other tips and thoughts. If there is more than one performance in a day, what are you going to do between shows?

Christopher Biggins once explained, "I never go out in between matinée and evening shows. I stay in the make-up. I have something to eat, go to sleep, and when I wake, I just tart up the make-up."

He is absolutely right of course. It is vital that the illusion should never be shattered. If the Dame pops out in civvies but with his make-up on or wearing his costume minus the wig, he will soon be spotted and that can ruin the whole illusion as well as spoiling the fun for any children you might catch a glimpse of you.

That does not just aply to Dames of course – a circus clown

would not be seen in only part of his make-up and costume or indeed even an international opera singer would not be seen in half a costume if he was appearing at La Scala. The same applies to Dame Nelly Telly at the Rotherham Civic.

Mentioning Christopher Biggins, he is a great example of taking your work seriously and also said, "I like to wear a different costume every entrance. A man my size is wonderful to see in different costumes – I'm really just a clothes horse. You have to make sure that your costumes are not just funny but do not appear creased or dirty. There can be as much work in putting your costumes away after a show as there is in doing the performance!"

Once again, Christopher is right and that's another thing about your dressing room – if you have a room which is exclusively yours, make sure it has enough space and is as organised as possible for your quick changes and making sure that your costumes are well looked after. If you are sharing, watch out for flying tea cups or other accidental spills!

Making sure that everything you do is real quality and totally professional cannot be stressed enough.

Panto is no less an art form than anything else. It takes real dedication because you have to be multi-talented and able to sing, dance and act. It's a tradition and you have to understand that you are working with children from five to 95. Virtually no other form of theatre is keyed towards the whole family experience.

Dames are organised chaos. If you're having fun, people will have fun with you. It is always worth remembering that the tradition of the Dame is bigger than any individual.

Naming no names I have seen someone cast as a Dame simply because he has been seen on a reality TV show. He knows nothing about panto or being a Dame and many think that all you have to do is put a dress on and just walk about like a man and shout at everyone. That is so not what it is all about.

Once an actor or comedy star has played Dame you will find that he is cast year after year as a Dame and loves every minute of it. That is not because he simply likes wearing a dress but because he has discovered the true essence of being a Dame and the fact that you are one of the best comedy characters ever created. The minute you walk on stage looking ridiculous but funny, the audience is yours and you can be friends with them for life because they will never forget you if you get it right.

Being a Dame is not just a job – it is a privilege.

CHAPTER ELEVEN

Once Upon A Time......

Are you sitting comfortably............? Sorry, old habits. If they are honest, no that's not a joke, don't interrupt. As I was saying, if they are honest any theatre manager will tell you that the annual pantomime is the most important show of the year. Not only do they want to make sure that their audiences have a great time but we are talking about the one show of the year that will produce more revenue than anything else. It can be a matter of life or death for some theatres and some production companies too. It is also usually the longest-running show of the year.

The thing is, how has it become so important and such a highlight on the calendar for both the theatre and local residents who will make up the audiences?

As far as I am concerned and most of us in fact, pantomime as we know it is a British invention. Some will probably dispute.that and they will point to other forms of entertainment from around Europe that were pantos of a sort in time gone by.

Apparently the word 'pantomime' comes not from the House of Parliament but from the Romans because the latin word 'pantomimus' . The Greeks will tell you that the Romans nicked it from them because they had a couple of words – 'panto' which means 'all' and 'mimos' which was a word for a dancer who acted loads of different parts.

However, let's not start another War of the Poses. The Greeks liked their dramas and the Romans liked their dramas too. Quite often those taking part didn't make it to 'pay day' but let's not go into that.

The Roman version was not just about what went on in the arenas, of course. Pantomimes were often performed in private houses and were a combination of music, singing, dancing, acting and comedy. That sounds more like it. Those shows were very popular of course and held in great esteem. I wonder what Latin is for "E's behind you!"

The Romans followed the Greeks into history and in the Middle Ages different sorts of panto-like entertainment were popular in different parts of Europe. In Italy they went for comedy drama with groups of actors touring the country to present all sorts of plays which had to contain a fair bit of comedy even if they were quite emotional dramas. Along came Harlequin to help things along and a genre was born.

Meanwhile in England, groups of Mummers were going around, often putting on shows of George and the Dragon, especially at Christmas time. Now we're getting somewhere. What better than George and the Dragon for "if you see the dragon children, you will give me a shout, won't you?" Yes, indeed. George hears about the beautiful princess whose dad – the king – wants her to marry someone brave enough to rid the land of the cursed dragon. George applies for the job. Moving swiftly away from the acceptable script, enter Captain Hook who is determined that he will marry the princess and take over the king's role and wealth. He tried to nobble George but gets eaten by the dragon. George then beats the dragon in a penalty shoot-out and they all live happy ever after. Throw in a bit of slapstick cake making in the palace kitchen and a dame in the form of the princess's old nanny (well, not that old, if you don't mind) and what have you got – Pantomime!!!

Yes, those mummers knew a thing or two. They became more and more popular and as William Shakespeare and others started making theatres and plays even more popular, it is not difficult to see how the whole idea of panto started to take off.

During the 16th to 18th century there were rival theatre companies, especially in London. Some actually had a theatre but many appeared in the courtyards of inns, sweeping the horse manure to one side so that the spectactors had somewhere to stand

and watch. The more affluent mem,bers of the audience were accommodated in galleries which were actually balcony walkways leading to some of the rooms to let in the inn.

The various groups did their best to outdo each other in drama productions and most had at least one comedy star, almost a jester, who delivered the funny lines, danced and did a few acrobatics. He was written into most scripts. The audiences were usually pretty enthusiastic and did not mind too much if the rain was falling heavily just so long as the production was worth seeing. If it wasn't they soon let the actors know exactly what they thought of it including later on in the inn itself where both actors and adiences would either celebrate or drown their sorrows.

Lincoln's Inn Theatre and the Theatre Royal, Drury Lane were two of the most bitter rivals and were constantly trying to beter each other during the early 18th century. They fell into a pattern of producing drama offerings which always including a comedy section, usually at the end, following the traditional showbiz rule of 'Send 'em 'ome 'appy".

It was this ethos which led to the 'Tavern Bilkers' at Drury Lane which was probably the nearest thing to today's pantomime. It was not especially well received and was not repeated for a while.

You can't keep a good panto down though and gradually the idea of such a production crept back in and what resembled pantos started to be performed around London and then in the provinces. The titles would be unrecognisable today as this was long before Peter Pan flew across the stage or the Seven Dwarfs got the beards in a tangle.

The pantos were different as well because there was a lot of mime in most of them and very little dialogue. The comedy was greatly visual but the comedy lines started to be included until pantos developed into an all-singing, all-dancing performance with good guys, bad guys, beautiful ladies and, of course, eventually the Dame.

We have touched on this already but men – well, mostly boys – dressed as young women in plays produced centuries ago. Ironically it was ballet that really introduced the principal boy being played by a girl as there was a bit of a shortage of male dancers who could be as elegant as the young ladies. That's another story though. Well, almost because it is worth mentioning that in the first half of the 19th century there was a lady called Madame Vestris and she often played the parts of young men in operas. She was quite a gal because most women appeared on stage in long dresses but her Madameship often wore shorts and – dare I say this – showed her legs from mid-thigh down. The hussy!!! Needless to say she was very popular with the men in the audiences and was showered with flowers and invitations night after night, a real 19th Century sex symbol.

Later on stars like Vesta Tilley and Marie Lloyd also made a huge success of playing principal boy in panto.

I was working on stage in panto with Cannon and Ball at Lincoln Theatre Royal a few years ago. Believe it or not they were playing the Ugly Sisters in Cinderella. I was the Dame and Prince Charming and Dandini were played by girls. Bobby Ball stopped the show at one stage and said to the packed audience, "Look at us (Ugly Sisters) and look at them (Principal Boys). We blokes playing women and their girls playing blokes. Is panto sick or what?"

He was joking of course and the audience roared with laughter but when you really think about it – it is no wonder that some people are 'confused.'!

So Dames in the panto sense began to appear around about the 1820s and these days you can't really have a panto without a Dame.

As for the pantomimes themselves well the most popular is Cinderella of course. In the 19th century Cinderella was a huge panto which lasted about four hours.

These days it usually runs for about an hour and a half plus the interval which is usually aimed at fifteen minutes but if the ice cream queue is slow can also run to twenty or more minutes.

These days pantos are shorter because they are mostly aimed at familiies with young children and it is considered that the attention span of children is not as long as it used to be. I'm not sure about that – I think if you goive everyone a great show they lose track of time and don't want it to end.

Anyway, Cinderella is without a doubt the most popular and virtually guarantees good audiences for a lengthy season. There are usually two Dames in Cinderella – namely the ugly sisters but sometimes there is a third Dame who is a Nanny or something along those lines. The Ugly Sisters are not really funny characters and the comedy is often down to Buttons but if you have a good role for a comedy Dame then the fun possibiities are increased of course.

Snow White and the Seven Dwarfs is also hugely popular and the Dame character is written in especially for the extra comedy potential. Her name varies from panto to panto and can simply be Dame Betty or something a little more exotic such as Dame Dolly Dumpling.

It is good if you can keep the same Dame name no matter which panto you are in but if the scriptwriters need you to have a particular name of their invention, then you just go with it.

In Snow White the Dame can be anything from Snow White's Nanny to a woodman's wife.

Peter Pan is a fantastic – or Pantastic – panto and the Dame has always been either the children's Nanny or Captain Hook's ship's cook.

The Dame is so much a part of traditional pantomime that even if the story line does not lend itself to the presence of a comedy female, the scriptwriters will cleverly find a way to include one – just ask anyone who has been in Robinson Crusoe.

Jack and the beanstalk is not a problem because Jack's mother is usually the Dame and there is a lot of fun to be had between Jack and his 'Mum' and even the panto cow who is traded for the magic beans. If the Dame is good on visual comedy, her attempt at milking the cow can be a brilliant opportunity for genuine hilarity.

Sleeping Beauty sometimes has a Nanny and sometimes has a fairy godmother character who is played as a Dame. Either way it is an excellent panto whether you are a Dame or a villain. Just remember that if you are thinking of embarking upon a career as a Dame, you will never play the heroine and thus you will never get woken up by a kiss from the handsome prince – male or female!

Of course, Aladdin's mother is a brilliant character for a Dame just as in Jack and the Beanstalk and the comedy is limited only by the imagination of those involved.

Even Dick Whittington includes a Dame. How? Well, as we have said before a cook can be dropped into any script and the slapstick just falls into place along with the verbal gags and a comedy song or two.

Both John Inman and Danny La Rue were popularly cast in Mother Goose which is another very popular panto and quite a classic really. The story is very old and it is the tale of Mother Goose and her son Jack who buys a goose which lays a golden egg. Jacks sells the goose to a dishonest merchant, Mother Goose turns Jack into Harlequin and his ladyfriend into Columbine, The egg is thrown into the sea and a fish brings it back. The merchant threatens to kill the goose but Mother Goose catches it and climbing onto its back flies up to the moon.

So, it has all the ingredients, the good guys, the bad guy, the Dame, everything. John Inman once described it as he Hamlet of pantos. It's a rare panto because the Dame is actually the central character. The actual goose is often called Priscilla while her owner, the Dame is often just called Mother Goose or, in some pantos she has been called Gertie Goose and a whole range of other comedy names – all repeatable!

Mother Goose is probably not one of the first panto ttles that would spring to mid in a pub quiz but it always works well because of having a great comedy central character plus a real villain, a slightly gormless but loveable son and, of course, the cuddly goose.

The panto storyline has changed a fair but from the very original but it is a lot of fun.

Beauty and the Beast has always been a popular panto too. Disney did a great job with this story but it is always worth remembering that these stories were pantos long before Disney came on the scene.

Robin Hood often features in Babes In The Wood and has also had special pantos written around the character.

Babes in the Wood is all about a boy and his sister being abandoned in the woods by their wicked uncle – sometimes the Sheriff of Nottingham. When you think about it, a lot of panto stories border on being horror stories! Anyway, they face all sorts of dangers but Robin Hood or another handy hero, gets his Merrie Men together and saves the children. They all live happily ever after of course.

Goldilocks and the Three Bears is another great favourite. Mind you, I have seen a few dark-haired Goldilocks in my time and I have even seen Goldilocks and the Bears which does not specify how many bears which in turn means that the producers can save money by having just two bears! Goldilocks often has a circus theme too which means that there is a need for speciality acts such as jugglers, acrobats, plate-spinners and so on. Often there were animal acts too but, sadly, modern thinking has banished the TV chimps and other wonderful animals from gracing the panto stage.

Pinnochio is still popular as well and is also well-off for characters as is Rapunzle which is quite a rare panto production these days but still seen occasionally.

Whatever the panto there are certain ingredients that are absolutely vital.

Audience participation is a 'must'. Most panto audiences need no invitation to cheer, boo and laugh but they want to do more than that so if one of the cast invited them to greet him every time he walks on stage or if they spot the escaped gorilla, they just love it.

To be honest it is not just the audience that loves it, the cast do as well. Hearing all that noise coming from the auditorium gives you a real lift and spurs you on to perform even begtter and perhaps even throw in a few extra gags to help the panto party go with a swing.

The jokes have got to be right. I have never liked it when the cast starts going into a batch of 'in-jokes' that only they understand. The audience have paid good money to be entertained not to watch the cast entertaining each other.

The jokes for a panto should never be smutty either. A very slight innuendo here and there is OK but it has to be clever so that the grown-ups can have a laugh on their level and the kids can have a laugh on their level. Everyone's happy. The kids are not left to ask to have the joke explained and the grown-ups do not have to give embarrassing answers.

Traditional circus clowning sets a great example for visual and verbal comedy. A clown will walk into the ring and say, 'Has anyone seen anybody looking for anyone?" It is complete nonsense yet could be a real question. Either way it gets a laugh just as a quick walk-round with an invisible dog. The clown can make it seem that the dog (the lead and collar are visible of course) keeps stopping to do what dogs do and if done properly it can be a very simple and funny routine.

That is the same formula that works in panto. A Dame can walk on crying very loudly. Another character joins the Dame and asks what is wrong. The Dame cries even more without saying anything coherent. You can bring on the whole cast eventually with them all in tears and saying things like 'Poor Gertie she must have had some very bad news'. Eventually of course, she blurts out that she has been peeling onions and gets chased off the stage. Daft – but it works.

Some good and well-known songs are important. The audience loves being able to clap, stamp their feet or join in the chorus so some popular songs are useful for that and maybe a ballad for the love-lorn handsome prince and another for the princess. The Dame needs a good comedy song of course but again, the lyrics need to be right for a family audience.

There should be some good slapstick as well. Chase scenes are always great fun but they need to be well choreographed otherwise the audience just gets bewildered at what on earth is going on.

Slosh routines – custard pies and so on – also need to be well rehearsed to get the timing right. Poor timing can ruin the whole thing and there is another point about using slosh – there has to be a point to it. If a character walks on and shovesd a custard pie intosomeone else's face it might be slightly amusing but it is far better if the character walks on with the custard pie visible to the audience but hidden from the other character who is showing off in some way. Now there is a point to the person getting the custard pie in the face – he is showing off. The audience have seen the custard pie and are in on the secret so the anticipation is building. What we need now is the unexpected. Just as the show-off turns to see what is happening, another character – perhaps even a female – walks on. The custard pie is launched, the show-off ducks and the innocent character gets it in the face.

Norman Wisdom was one of the greatest exponents of slapstick in the entire history of slapstick and he always said that the whole episode must be plausible – it could just happen. It should never just be a custard pie or cream for its own sake and the timing has to be spot-on. If you don't get it right your audience will be disappointed and laugh to be polite rather than because they cannot help themselves.

It is rare that you get a panto without a Dame and it is quite rare that you get a Dame without a panto. The two go together like Beauty and the Beast – I'll leave you to decide which is which!

CHAPTER TWELVE

A Dame At Home

What do the neighbours think? I have been asked that question a few times. How do they like living next door to a bloke who spends half his working life in a frock? Good question. So, what do the neighbours think? I guess that doing what I do is second nature to me I never give it a second thought. It's just always been that way and perfectly normal to me. Oh yes, it is!!!

We have distant neighbours – in that they are nice people who keep themselves to themselves and are happy for others to be the same. Of course we might just say 'hello' or wave at them as we put the bins out. No, I don't wear a frock to put the bins out!!!

There is an exception in that next door to us there is a lovely lady called Carol who has a keen interest in variety as it was and is very knowledgeable on the subject. We always have a chat about what I'm doing next or what I've done last week and so on. At the moment she is eagerly awaiting the publication of this book! So Carol, you have a mention. The other side of us we have neighbours who you can tell have no interest what so ever in variety or pantomime that's just how they are. When we first moved into our house we chatted over the back garden fence Norman Evans style but the guy next door who obviously fancied himself as a comedian kept weaving old stock gags into our conversation, which at first amused me a little. After a while his gags got on my nerves a bit and when the conversation came to, 'and what do you do for a living?' I just said, "Oh this and that you know."

It wasn't until I'd finished the panto season in Truro with Rick

Wakeman and the frocks had to be washed and were flapping in the wind on the clothes line that he sussed it all out – he doesn't do gags now.

I talk a lot about costumes and props because they are so very important. Every entertainer has something that helps him or her stand-out. Singers might have some favourite suits or dresses (the girls that is – I am not talking about dames right now – pay attention!). Some entertainers will carry a musical instrument with them, even one they can't pay. It is a prop that makes them different or gives them confidence, a bit like having a Teddy Bear with you.

Think about some of the stars you have liked and the little props or gimmicks they have had which makes them stand out – Val Doonican was known for his sweaters, Bernie Winters had a dog with him after he split from his brother Mike, Doddy had his tickling sticks, Jimmy Edwards had his huge moustache, Sandie Shaw didn't wear any shoes, Englebert Humperdink had his name, the list goes on and on.

You can have all the talent in the world but always remain in the background because you haven't had an ace card to get you really noticed and remembered. So costumes and props can be very special.

Of course, all that is for your work. At home, the Dame, like any other entertainer, is just another ordinary bloke who may like a pint at the pub, to go to a football match or watch soaps on television. It can be quite good fun to see a poster of yourself in a shop window and then when you go into the shop nobody knows it is you theyr are helping to promote.

One thing I never do is point to a poster and say, "That's me, you know – I am that Dame."

That would be unprofessional, could spoil the illusion, or worse, you might find the shopmanager asking you out for a date!

My latest seven or eight panto seasons have been with Cannon & Ball in my home town at Lincoln Theatre Royal. As in this case I'm kind of 'following myself' – an old circus term from legendary clown Jacko Fossett – so every year I would create new costumes accompanied by huge funny head-dress props and other bits and pieces. Of course i then transported them to the theatre in my car. Our across-the-road neighbour Yvonne, a lovely lady, once asked me ..."When are you taking your frocks to the theatre?" Then she admitted, "We wait for it every year for a sneak preview."

I was quite touched by that but it shows that you never know who's watching you. I suppose non-showbiz people find me a bit of an eccentric. For instance, whilst making costumes and larger-than-life hats you do, of course, need to try them on. One day I was making a panto prop in the front room like you do, assisted by my young daughter Beatrice who at the time must have been about 10 or 11 ... I'm dressed in a frock with big red spots on it plus dame boots (one Red One Yellow). Guess what? Of course, the doorbell rings and it's the window cleaner collecting his money. The look on his face when I opened the door got a 10 pound note from the drawer and without hesitation put the money in his hand and said "Merry Christmas, thank you very much!" was a picture. It's only now, on thinking about it that it must have looked very strange to him, but I guess I was that busy I had no time for inhabitations.

We have a large garden and I have a large garage which is also my workshop where I create all my props, costumes and other show things. Some costumes are a mixture of a frock and a prop so this is where the engineering training comes in handy. I once made a dame frock that made me look as if I was in the middle of a table with cups saucers around me. The frock part is fairly simple but a little more thought needs to go into how the table effect can be created. You need the table big enough for the audience at the back of the circle to be able to see so it needs to be large but light and practical, in that you need to be able to get through tabs or stage sets. My neighbours have seen me flitting from the workshop to the patio with proto type designs of all kinds of weird props ranging from a saw cut through my head to an exploding washing machine.

For many years I would watch panto dames come down the treads on the finale tottering whilst trying to balance a headdress, I always promised myself that I would not struggle like that. With my wigs and headdresses I've gone to a lot of trouble but it is well worth it because I can actually run or even skip down the treads, giving out comic energy. Most of my wigs are secured on a fibreglass cap so when you are wearing it there is no problem, it just feels snug and comfortable.

It necessitates in making a Red Head that's a replica of your head in plaster. First you need to make a mould of your head then transfer it into the Red Head. From this you can make fibreglass caps that fit exactly to the contours of your head. On these you can fit a range of fixtures and fittings including wires to control eyes that wink etc. etc. When you make an entrance the head needs to be up straight because if not it spoils the gag or effect.

The audience needs to have confidence in your props too. If not the focus on what could go wrong. They start to think, "Oh it's going to fall off." While they are worrying about that, they are not laughing!

Of course, when things do look as if they have gone wrong that can be very funny but it is a lot funnier if you are controlling it because you can 'place the gag' as in a cod corpse or trip.

In my variety act I do a 'Cod Vent routine' that's a ventriloquist act were my lips move and that goes terribly wrong at the end. Before I performed this I practised and practised with the music so that the leg of the dummy fly's around my neck at precisely the right moment because that's where the laugh is and that is where the laugh will always be.

In one panto a few years ago one of the characters ran onyo the stage, slipped and fell over. It actually hurt him but everyone else thought this was so funny – especially the audience (that's very important) that we convinced him to keep it in for the entire run.

On another occasion there was a comedy car. One of the cast leaned over it a little too far just as a jet of flame shot up. He quickly backed off but it caught his wig alight. He wasn't aware of it until someone from the wings rushed on and put him out with a fire extinguisher. The audience was in tears of laughter but he refusedto do it at every performance. Spoil sport!

It's important to look after your panto props because hidden within those props are all the laughs you'll ever need to be a success in a panto production. All my props and frocks and I've got quite a few, are always washed after the panto and dried on the washing line, which makes them fresh. Then they are put in plastic boxes ready for storage in the attic. I must confess when we have had the odd workman in to do a job, they come down from the attic a little dazed after seeing ventriloquist dolls' heads hung from the rafters, prop legs and arms in skips and large wigs with giant washing powder boxes on them.

It is not just the dame props because I like to use props in my variety and cabaret acts. For quite a few years I starred in a wartime show called WE'LL MEET AGAIN. It was produced and promoted by my friend of 40, years Duggie Chapman. This show toured every year from March to October sometimes working seven days a week.

Duggie was great for me because he loved variety and if I had an idea for his show he was quick to listen. In the wartime show I was presented at the very beginning and then did the 'warm up' five to six minutes. That was the best length for a warm-up because it gets the show going, gets the audience settled and leaves them looking forward to the acts to follow. Later in the performance I would close the first half, usually with impersonations of stars from the war years.

In the second half we always did a 'sketch' and one of my favourites was the lamp-post sketch. In the old days the lamp-post sketch was done with the comic and a pretty show girl. The girl is dressed as 'a lady of the night' leaning on a lamp-post looking for trade. The comic comes along and offers her money, normally starting with one note then two. The lady of the night shakes her head to signify "No" until the comic produces all his money (a big wad). She nods, smiles and quickly takes the money. The 'customer' rubs his hands with delight and steps forward. The girl moves out of the way and the comic takes the lamppost. Audiences usually love it because they have one thing in their mids and it turns out that he is after something else.

Yes a funny sketch but how do you get a lamppost into the boot of a Ford Focus? This was solved by using an umbrella and having the girl signify it was raining! This worked rather well and was a neat portable prop.

On a touring version of the show there are no dancers so we

had to use the only female we had which was the female vocalist. The sketch now ran like this: Girl walks on and sings a few bars of the song Lilly Marline then puts her hand out as if it's raining and puts up the umbrella. On comes Steve dressed as a rather drunken sailor. He sees the girl, smiles knowlingly at the audience and goes through the offering the money bit until the girl agrees, takes themoney and hands him the umbrella.

It sounds simple, doesn't it but one day Lucia Matees is in tears in the wings as the sketch is about to run. Why? She's forgotten the umbrella!!!! With seconds to go I rush to the dressing room and grab a head scarf I'd used in my spot. I said to Lucia all in a rush 'put the head scarf on love and use that instead'. Half a second later she's on stage sings the song, the sketch gets a big laugh and Uncle Steve wins again. What a 'good little pro' Lucia was. There was no panic, she just got on with it and that's probably down to Lucia's pedigree in showbiz as her grandfather was a funny comic by the name of Frankie Holmes Her father and uncle were also both in showbiz. Some of the modern luvvies think they have invented improvisation! It's been around for centuries.

I have always promised myself that if I ever do that sketch again with an umbrella, I'll make it so that as the 'customer' walks off with his purchase it starts to rain – under the umbrella!

The moral of these stories are simply that props and costumes are so very, very important and should be cherished.

Yes, someone driving behind you seeing some strange costumes, wings and props on your back seat might wonder what in earth they are following but that doesn't matter. Don't try to squeeze your costumes out of sight, cover them over if you are worried about theft and make sure your car is locked – many performers have suffered at the hands of thieves stealing from their cars. Strange really – why would a passing thief want to steal a bright orange wig?

Don't worry about your neighbours either. They will soon get used to seeing you both in costumes and in civvies. They might think you are a little crazy but then they are probably right, don't you think?

CHAPTER THIRTEEN

Bits And Pieces

I t is rare that two days are the same even if you are in a long panto or summer season and that makes it constantly alive. Things go wrong or they go right and you have to deal with it. It is a rollercoaster ride. The characters you meet are also a miscellany of personalities. All of that contributes to a way of life that is pretty unique and it also means that you are not a bad guest at a dinner party becaue you have so many ales to tell – all varied.

Let me tell you about Duggie Chapman – a legend. It must have been a good 15 years after the panto with Frank Carson and Roy Barraclough at the Charter Theatre, Preston that Duggie Chapman rang me, completely out of the blue. It was a pleasant surprise and it got better as the conversation went on.

I had just finished a summer season for Trafford and Parnell – that is Tommy Trafford and Ronnie Parnell, very well known in the business – at Whitby. It was a fairly exhausting season as we did three different shows a week. It was actually quite enjoyable because that kind of production keeps you on your toes and I found it very satisfying to have risen to the challenge each week.

Anyway, the phone rang and Duggie Chapman's voice was at the other end. After the usual, "Hello Steve, how are you?" It's funny how people do that whether it is on the phone or when you bump into them at a theatre. They never actually listen. I often feel like answering, "Terrible. My wife ran off with the Harlem Globetrotters, my cat has been taken into space by a green alien and I died three days ago." I'm sure the answer would , "Oh, good, good, nice to hear you're getting on alright."

121

Duggie asked me 'what my act' was at the moment. Which one? I had just been doing several acts at Whitby and I was also doing clubs which often called for a variation of act night after night.

I just said, "Oh this and that."

Duggie then said, "I hear you do Max Miller and Tessie O'Shea these days?"

"Yes I said," and the next thing I knew I was duly booked by Duggie to do a gig at Grange-over-Sands near Morecambe. I knew that it would be a bit of a trial run because if I didn't go well I probably wouldn't hear from Duggie again. As it happened and thank goodness, I paralysed them. No, I'm not blowing any trumpets, it was hard work and had talen me about 40 minutes to win them over!!!!

Later I was indeed booked again by Duggie, this time for a summer season in Skegness and Southport , on opposite coasts of course. This time we agreed on length of spots and so on, a definite improvement on my previous outing for Duggie where I had to just play it by ear – meaning that if someone shouted, "Gerrofff!", it was time for me to end my act.

The audiences that Duggie's music hall shows attracted were far different from the clubs I had worked for what already seemed like a lifetime. In the music hall shows your act had to be clean and you had to register with the audience in the first 30 seconds as the spots were only around 12 mins.

I must say at this stage that if someone has to totally rely on bad language and filth to get a reaction from the audience then they are not really a great entertainer. They cater for a certain type of audience but then so does a loud-mouth in the local pub. The talent of being an entertainer is to make people laugh without any sort of offence, to sing songs in a way that makes people feel happy or perhaps sad but never offended.

Each to their own of course, but non-family entertainment has never appealed to me either as a performer or as a member of an audience.

Well, that summer season proved to be something of a launching pad because I then toured with Duggie's shows for the next 30 years. If Duggie liked what you did he kept you on! I had lots of adventures with Duggie as he was a likeable rogue, taught me lots of stuff I would never have learned in clubs.

One of the best bits of advice was always do your strongest spot first, then you have the audience for the rest of the show. Both Duggie and Beryl Johnson, his partner, once sat me down in Duggie's Jaguar and gave me a master class in communication with the audience. As I'm from Lancashire I was working the gags in a strong Lancashire accent (for warmth) which worked in Lancashire of course and even in Yorkshire but elsewhere they could not understand me! Duggie suggested instead of 'I've not bin well', change to 'I've not been very well' still Lancashire but understandable to all! A slight change but it worked.

I applied this advice to everything I said and it worked a treat so, thank you Duggie. I was so lucky to meet Duggie as he introduced me to lots of old pros including Jacko Fossett, a great clown from the circus, and his wife Connie of the Read Twins variety act. I would always stay at Jacko's house at North shore Skegness when playing Skeggy and we would have late night chats about the business etc. I literally soaked up Jacko's tips and tricks like a sponge.

Here's another tip – because all these wonderful pros could tell I was listening they went further and told me more! If you seem uninterested they just clam up. Who can blame them? – they are giving a free education, the best people in the business giving you free lessons – who wouldn't want to listen?!

There will always be a special place in my heart for Duggie Chapman. He showed that he believed in me! Either that or I was just working cheap at the time!

As well as great characters and odd experiences this business presents you with many challenges – especially from the weather. Allow me to explain what happened once in 1977.

It was a dark and a freezing night...no it wasn't, not yet anyway. Harry Rawden, my manager of Derick Rawden Management, was a great hustler (term used for good agents). Harry had secured me a week's work in Scotland for legendary agent and promotor Andy Green. The week started on a Sunday noon – at a place called Billy's Bar in Musselburgh but Harry had also put me into a night club in Cumbria the Friday and Saturday before with a lovely girl vocalist called Jerry Benton.

As I had no driving licence I had to either take the train or risk a heavy fine if I drove my own car! I opted for the insane route – a la Macbeth – the insane root to which Banquo refers is a herb causing madness. It probably refers specifically to hemlock or henbane, both deadly. Banquo asks Macbeth if they have mistakenly eaten some poison that "takes reason prisoner" (makes them lose their minds) because the Witches vanish into thin air. For my purpose it just meant I had to catch trains at ungodly hours carry props and music plus a banjo uke!

OK, so this week for Andy Green in Scotland really started by waiting for the post train around 4.30 am on the freezing cold Workington station. When it arrived I went from a cold bench to get seated eventually on an even cooler old British Rail train.

By about 10.00 am we were pulling into the station at Glasgow. First of all I had to look for a trolley for my baggage as I endured the bit I dreaded – 'changing platforms'. I looked for a trolley with no success then behind me I heard a thick Glaswegian accent say 'Ayah look-in for a trolley Son'? Before I could answer the Porter who must have been hiding around the corner had all my baggage on his trolley which cost me a few quid I can tell you.

Later the second freezing cold train chugged in to Edinborough city and this time I found a trolley. Then I looked for the taxi rank which seemed in a dark place of the station in those days. I asked the cab driver if he could take me to Billy's bar Musselburgh he replied "Ayah sure Son?" I said, "Oh yes I'm the lunchtime cabaret today." The cab driver replied, "Good luck with that one Son!" He never even smiled!

We soon arrived at Billy's Bar where my name was on a large poster in the foyer billed as 'Britain's funniest comedian'. Even before I went on stage I thought the billing slightly over exaggerated!!!! The time came for my spot and by this time I felt as if someone had thrown salt into my eyes, I was so tired. To say the spot didn't go well would be an understatement. It was a tough lunchtime audience and all they were interested in really was a few pints and their Sunday dinner. Except for one guy who heckled "If you're funny, Crippen was innocent!!!" They didn't even laugh at him so I felt slightly reassured.

I was staying at Mrs Robinson's who supplied pro digs in Musselburgh. I was in the foyer looking for a taxi number on the board when an argument started. There was a guy slapping his wife around the face and sticking the boot in. I intervened, saying "Excuse me mate, there's no need for that!" Just then the woman reared up to me in her broad Scottish dialect fuming with drink . She retorted, "Leave him alone, he's been in the War yi know!"

Just then I was rescued by a kindly lady who sayis, "Come with me sonny ... you won't get a taxi now luv, where are you heading?" I explained that I was hoping to go to Mrs Robinsons on Corporation Road. "OK," she said,"No problem."

She carried my Uke and I carried the rest. As we walked towards the car park I noticed she had a 'Club foot' (too many catalogues, I thought ...old gag). I asked her which was her car she replied "Oh that's mine over yonder, the light blue one." The only car I could see that was light blue was an invalid car! How we managed to get the props in I'll never know but we did and I soon arrived exhausted at Mrs Robinsons, God bless that kind lady who ever she was.

During the week for Andy Green I was sent to various working men's clubs and, to be honest, I 'died' at most of them. My confidence was waning fast. One of the very worst ones was performing at what I've now learned as the social board at a Masonic lodge. The Masonic brethren had all had so much to drink that during my act some on the top table put down their heads on the table and fell asleep.

I could not help myself and said, "I'll recall this night one day on Parkinson." A voice from the crowd shouted, "Oh no you won't ... believe me, you're not going on Parkinson sonny."

The end of that week could not come fast enough for me. On the Friday all Andy's acts for the week were summoned to his office in Musselburgh town centre for payment. My name was shouted and I duly presented myself. In the office were Andy's wife was giving out the cash. Before Andy's wife handed over my money she looked over her glasses at me with a stern face and said, it's been a tough week for you Stevie I know but you persevered and that's good." Then she went on, "Your act is good BUT not strong enough for our venues; you have loads of talent Son BUT yi dinna know what to do with it!"

On recollection she had hit the nail right on the head. She knew the business alright and to their credit they had not paid me off.

The last gig was Saturday but high up in the Highlands, I was to travel with a guitar vocalist, do the gig then catch the last train back to Manchester. Simple. No, it was far from simple. Remember, this was Scotland – the North of Scotland.

It started off as planned but as we made our way to the club, the snow got thicker and thicker and we only just managed to get the car into the car park. By the time of the gig the guitar vocalist Johnny Dean and I had become great friends as Andy Green had put us together on a few gigs during the week. Although it was snowing fast the club was packed to the rafters. The plan was for me to open with a short spot put Johnny on for a while and then I would do forty minutes of gags and so on before the interval after which Johnny would finish with a big rock and roll spot.

That night went brilliantly and as the laughs came thick and fast I kept thinking why could Andy Green not see me now on top form? By the end of the night the snow was so thick we could not move the car. Johnny made an announcement, "Can anyone take Steve and me in for the night." "Yes!" Came the shouted reply from a small guy called Billy at the back of the club. "Come with me."

By around mid-night we were sat by a huge fire in Billy's house having a great time entertaining him with our showbiz stories of life on the road. I think in those days B&Bs were around £15 per night so we had done well to be guests of this nice man. Johnny and I slept in the same room and agreed that in the morning we would treat Billy for his kindness.

When the morning came, the snow had melted enough to move the car and for us to get on our way. As we made our goodbyes to Billy and his wife Johnny and myself had a crisp £10 note each in our pockets as per our discussion, intended to give it to Billy on our exit.

"Well thank you for last night Billy," we both thanked him and shook his hand ... Then Johnny said "How much do we owe you?" Billy replied in his magnificent Stanley Baxter dialect, "Oh it will just be £30 pounds each if you don't mind ... as you did have two whiskeys each of you." We still thanked him for his generosity but if I'd have known I would have had another whisky or two!

Scotland in the snow can be an expensive experience!

I am starting to feel cold just thinking about it again so let us head for a warmer tale from sunny Torquay.

I have mentioned Torquay before of course but I did not mention the experience I am about to reveal. These are the sort of crazy things that are done and said in this business no matter whether you are a stand-up comic, a singer, dancer, juggler or even a Dame.

This was a summer season so I was not a Dame, I was Steve Barclay. Who??? Yes, that just about sums it up.

My flat for the summer was in a large house on Daddyhole Plain, quite a swish area of Torquay and overlooking the sea. Brilliant Manchester comedian Eddie Grant or Eddie P. Allen as he was then (not by choice as he owed money everywhere) also had a flat in the house.

By 1976 Eddie was, I suppose, classified as an alcoholic or at least a very heavy drinker. He certainly had some eccentric ways, probably enough to fill a book of his own. As an example when you are doing a long summer season the time comes for the Wimbledon tennis champioonships. It doesn't make much difference to most of us because we are there to do our job and the audiences turn up no matter what is on television. So, one day we all realised that it was the start of Wimbledon. Eddie approached me and said, "Come to town with me Steve, I need a telly to watch the tennis."

"Ok," I said. "Let's go." Withour further ado we got into his blue car and off we went. Actually I describe it as blue but one side was a kind of silver as he had used it against the side of walls to navigate his way home from a few of his gigs. Why? Think about it – I'm surprised the police didn't – well, not often anyway.

To my alarm I could smell strong drink as we drove into town but we made it without actual mishap although there were a few expressions of panic on the faces of some of the other drivers. So we end up in the Co-op electrical section looking at TVs. Eddie was always asking Trevor George for subs, – that was not uncommon in this business in those days. Eddie's wages were £150 per week while mine were £100.

So, Eddie asked the assistant how much the TV was – after he had looked at the price tag of course. The lady answered as per the price tag – £140.00 (which was a fortune in those days). Eddie tried to persuade her to give him a discount, even in exchange for a couple of tickets fore the show. The lady was not for turning though and Eddie really did want that television. It would probably have been cheaper for him to go to Wimbledon and watch the tennis live!

Eddie had no alternative than to ask me to lend him £2.00 as he only had £138.00 left from his wages which had been given to him the day before. I handed him the £2.00 reminding him to be careful because he had the rest of the week to go before the next pay-day and there were little things like food to be considered. Eddie's reply was, "Steve are you stupid or what?... How am I going to watch Wimbledon without a telly?"

We duly carted the TV into the boot of his 'Silver and Blue car' and set off around the winding narrow streets of Torquay. Eddie had already bumped a few lamp posts and was driving up a one-way street. A man passing by shouted to us in his West Country accent, "Here can you not see this is a one way street'!" ... Eddie wound the window down and retorted, "We're only going one way – sod off!"

Since then I've heard so many other legendary stories about Eddie like the time he was playing a week for Duggie Flood, a Manchester night club owner, who owned the Northern Club. The week started on a Sunday night with a band call at around four in the afternoon. About eleven in the morning Duggie received a call from Eddie, phoning from a coin box. Eddie explained to Duggie he's stuck in Bournemouth and his car is a right off so can't make the band call.

Duggie, being desperate for Eddie's services as a top audience-pulling comic in the Manchester club scene, told Eddie to get a taxi for which he will pay when Eddie arrived, then stop it from his wages.

About half past four that afternoon Eddie arrived in a taxi much to Duggie's relief. He staggered to the waiting Duggie and told him, "Duggie the taxi is £70 and his meter's still running. Duggie handed Eddie £75 and told Eddie to tip the driver.

The week was a huge success with Eddie 'ripping the audiences apart." At the of the week Duggie expressed his thanks to Eddie and informed him that because he had done so well and been a great crowd puller and pleaser he would not be taking the taxi money out of his wages.

A few weeks later Duggie had to get a taxi to the railway station and the driver asked Duggie how the comic went the other week? Puzzled, Duggie replied, "Which comic?" To which the taxi driver replied, "The one I brought from a pub in Salford the other Sunday!"

The best one by far came years later. Eddie was working a night club in Manchester and stayed back in the dressing room after the venue had been locked up. Eddie then proceeded to rob the fruit machines and help himself to some bottles of drink. He was about to leave with his ill-gotten gains when he was confronted by two Alsatian dogs crawling ferociously towards him. Eddie rang the police and explained what he had done and about the dogs.

Because Eddie was known for his comedy act, the policeman on duty laughed and simply said, "Look Eddie, you've had too much – just get to bed." Eddie pleaded with him, "No, no, no, no! I'm really here stuck in the club! I'll flash the lights on and off until you come so you can see I'm sober and telling the truth." Well, Eddie was telling the truth at least.

The police arrived and see the lights in the club flashing on and off. They had the dogs moved, arrested Eddie and he was given a six months jail sentence.

Six months later Eddie had completed his time as a guiest of Her Majesty and he ran up the club owner for a gig. The club owner could hardly believe it and responded, "You cheeky, hard-faced person!" – or words to that effect. However, after pleading more, Eddie did indeed get a comeback gig at the club. The night of his gig, the club was packed to the rafters with every comic or entertainer in Manchester all wondering what Eddie's opening line will be.

Well, there was a drum roll to get everyone's attention and then the compere simply said, "OK folks, its cabaret time! Please welcome – Eddie Grant!"

The band played Eddie on with 'When your smiling'. Eddie sauntered onto the typical club stage, puffed at his cigarette and looked at the crowd who were waiting with bated breath. Eddie did not disappoint them. He puffed at his cigarette a second time and in the silence, dryly said, "A funny thing happened to me last time I was here!!"

The crowd exploded into hysterical laughter, the drummer fell off his drum stool and Eddie won again.

CHAPTER FOURTEEN

Oh, Alright – More Pieces And Bits

Let's go back in time again – we have been here before but I spilled some of it the first time so let's go back and I'll mop it up a bit.

Junior Showtime was quite a big children's show of its time with a few spin-offs including Junior Hometime run by BBC Radio Manchester. I'd done a few Junior Home Time broadcasts for the BBC and was asked to appear on their radio Christmas Party, hosted by Tom Tyrel, a lovely guy who covered sports.

We recorded the show at the Hulme Hippodrome with a few hundred screaming kids. As I paced around the green room before I went on, there was also a young girl there with her mother. I'd just made my own way to the theatre as I was getting to be quite a seasoned little pro at 16 years.

The girl's mother said the normal, "Oh and where are you from luv?"

I mentioned I'd come from Oldham on the bus. The girl's mother told me her and her daughter were from Rochdale. The little girl was about seven years of age and already had a fabulous voice.She grew up to becoome quite an international star. Her name? Lisa Stansfield.

A while later when I was eighteen years of age I was booked to do a Sunday night show at Warrington Working Men's Club. It went alright and I stayed over in Warrington because early the next morning I had to go hot-foot with my suitcase of props in

131

hand to start a week's engagement in a theatre show called Junior Startime at the New Brighton Pavilion theatre (that's the old theatre which has since been redeveloped in 2008). The show was promoted by a mind-reading act called Jack Delmar from Weston-Super-Mare under the trading name of International Attractions. Jack appeared every inch the theatre gent insisting that the ladies went first at the Monday morning band call!

After the band call I walked with my suitcase along a street that was conveniently at the back of the theatre. It was convenient because there were lots of B&BS running along the street, perfect for anyone appearing at the theatre.

I tried a few of the B&Bs, each time enthusiastically saying. "Oh hello, my name's Steve Hutch and I'm appearing at the Pavilion Theatre in Junior Startime. I'm looking for accommodation for the week."

I was greeted with either. 'Well you're not staying here,' or just having the door slammed in my face! I tried again and again using the same patter until finally I was nearly dragged in by a lovely scouse-sounding lady called Mrs Flanagan. All the family were completely star struck. The next day Mrs F asked, "What time would you like to get up darling?"

"Oh whenever," I casually replied. She went further by asking if I liked tin tomatoes, I told her that I certainly did and so every day that week I rose late morning and polished off a large full breakfast with small tin of tomatoes, I didn't have the heart to say there were too many tomatoes. She was a lovely lady.

As I woke every morning not having to be in the theatre until the afternoon, I remember thinking ... 'This is the life for me.' In fact I was 26 before I knew what Cornflakes were. All the family came to the show later in the week and on the Saturday night after two shows I was asked by Mrs F to do the whole act again in her front room for the family and neighbours and friends. There were probably more in the audience in her front room than at the theatre!

There were no ladies on the bill of Junior Startime as, such as the name suggested. The acts and artistes were mostly young children who had appeared on YTV's Junior Showtime except for a young clarinet player called Karen Bawsley from St Anne's who formed part of a family group called The Dixie Land Jazz Kids. Later in the week I took Karen to the cinema, I don't know where it was but it was a long walk there and back, which suited me very well with this young blonde on my arm.

Jack Delmar's daughter was part of the double act they did called The Amazing Zandra. Interestingly Jack, dressed in evening suit, insisted on standing by the box office every night doing a sort of meet and greet. In actual fact he was looking into hand bags wallets and so on for objects he could call upon later in the stage act – The Amazing Zandra. For instance in what was a very slick mind-reading act, Jack would say, "There's a lady with a crocodile skin hand bag, in that hand bag is a pink compact ... am I correct'?" There would be a shriek from the lady and a round of applause from the crowd and so it went on.

Closing the first half of the show was recent new faces winner Malandra Newman who was at the time the youngest ever person to win TV's New Faces. I remember at the time she didn't seem to mix with the others and her parents kind of kept her in the dressing room all the time. This young lady later became Emmerdale Farm actress Malandra Burrows who played the part of Kathy Glover. The next time I met Malanda was years later after she had left Emmerdale and was on one of my very good friend Johnny Dennis's music Halls at the Leeds City Varieties Theatre. I introduced myself of course and recalled the week we did in 1974. Malanda just said, "No I'm afraid that wasn't me. I was never Malanda Newman." Even now I find this a strange thing to say but – as they say – that's showbiz!

I met a great guy also called Jack that week. This Jack had appeared on Opportunity Knocks as The Singing Dog and Jack... but this time he was with all his family to support his daughter Lesley who was using 'The singing dog' in her new act which they called Lesley and her TV Singing Dog. Jack and I stayed in communication for some years. When I come to think of it, I guess it must have been my name change to Steve Barclay that contributed to us losing touch.

Closing the show -almost always the considered 'star' of the performance – was nine times winner of Opportunity Knocks Steven Smith. He had apeared on Op Knocks as Steven Smith and Father. I am ashamed to say that I don't remember much about him because he seemed to spend nearly all his time in his dressing room with his dad. What i do recall though was that her went very well and after the TV appearances he was managed by the Trevcor George Agency of Torquay. Of course, years later Trevor George would be my manager too.

Going back to Jack Delmar for a while, it must be said that if he was a real mind reader he should have for seen that the houses were at times going to be atrocious. Sometimes thetre were only about 36 in this massive theatre. On the Saturday we did two shows at 6.30 and 8.40. Towards the end of the last shows Jack came into my dressing room and said, "Don't tell the others here's your money … you're a good pro Steve." With that he gave me a brown envelope with about £250 for the week. Later on I found out that I was the only act who was paid. Since then I have played New Brighton Pavilion many times with Danny La Rue and in the new theatre in We'll Meet Again and I'm thrilled to say that after all those years my old black and white photo (now yellow) is still in the bar, or it was the last time I played the theatre.

In the balmy summer of 1993 I found myself performing summer season in a show called The Good Old Days. It was indeed good but summer seasons days had changed since I remember them when I was a child in Blackpool in the 1960s. In Blackpool I remember seeing great stars like Arthur Haynes, Tessie O'Shea, Mike and Bernie Winters and a very young Jimmy Tarbuck who stole the show.

The show I was topping ran one night at the Southport Theatre then three nights in Skegness for Duggie Chapman productions. In the show was Mike Parkin, a ventriloquist and Paul Connor, a multi-instrumentalist who had worked with Charlie Cairoli as Paul the clown with a white face and a rather smart and sparkly Pierrot costume.

When in Skegness all the pros stayed at Jacko Fosset's house at Northshore close to the Northshore Golf Club. Jack was something of a legend in the business. I got on very well Jacko and I loved his brilliant stories from his days as a top of the bill circus clown. Jacko was married to one half of the double act called The Reed Twins who, because they were identical twins, had done a 'Mirror act' on the Moss Empire Variety circuit. The mirror act was simply a big picture frame with no glass stood in front of a black backcloth; because Connie and Marge were trained dancers they created a highly successful routine 'Mirroring' each other.

Every night while I was staying with Jacko I would be greeted at the door by him with a cheery smile and the words, "Hello Son, I've got your supper ready." By supper, Jack meant a large glass of whiskey! Jacko always had lots of fatherly advice like "Never get a big head … get a big pocket" or "Never drink and perform but have a good supper afterwards". Jacko's house was full of variety memorabilia including a large poster which covered the living room door of Jacko starring at the Blackpool Tower Circus.

By the time I met Jacko he wasn't working but still loved to talk about his days as a trampolinist high wire walker and of course his trade mark Jacko the clown. He once told me that he worked a lot with a young Tony Hancock on the Moss Empire circuit and gave Tony some straight advice. Apparently Jack had said, "Hank, give up son, go and work at your mother's guest house. This isn't for you."

Jacko always told me this story and finished it off by saying, "You see Steve, I just couldn't see him." Maybe it was Tony's new kind of comedy that puzzled Jacko. In jacko's lounge was a fantastic collection of videos of acts I'd never seen and lots of footage of Jacko at the Blackpool tower circus as well as some televised shows of him in Billy Smarts Circus.

One night Jacko said, "If you like variety comedy, watch this Son." it was a Scottish double act called Francie and Josie, also known as Ricky Fulton and Jack Milroy.

From their original opening song, 'I'd Rather Be Here With You' – written by Ricky Fulton at the Kings theatre Edinburgh – I was hooked right to the end of their act when they sang an up tempo version of 'So Long It's Been Good To Know You'.

Jacko knew all these variety people as friends and we usually stayed up chatting till the early hours about the heyday of variety.

I was soon in the record shops for copies of Francie and Josie's songs and routines which I soaked up like a sponge. I remember they wore smart Italian suits in bright colours which sat well against the hot footlights and bright tabs of the Kings Theatre, Edinburgh. As Jacko watched these with me, he said. "Take a look at these two – one has a red suit the other a blue suit, both against the yellow tabs ... make sure the audience can see you and you don't merge into the tabs behind you."

By 1995 I was touring for the second or third time with Danny La Rue and I remember we played dates in Scotland for a promotor called Robert C. Kelly. We played a week at the Kings Theatre, Edinburgh, a week at the Pavilion Glasgow then various other dates around Scotland including a one nighter at the Adam Smith Theatre in Kirkcaldy.

I had spoken to Danny many times about my liking of the Scottish comics Francie and Joise and, in particular Jack Milroy. Danny of course knew them both very well. As it was a Music Hall show I wore very heavy make-up and at the end of one performance I was 'washing off' when Danny's unmistakable theatrical voice shouted from his dressing room... 'Steve come and meet my friends'! Of course I was there in a shot and standing right there in front of me was Jack Milroy!

He had been in to see the show and as he shook my hand, he said, "Steve, I hate you -... you're so funny." We all laughed at his joke and chatted for a while. Danny looked at me with his mischievous smile and quipped, "You see love ... I know everybody." At that meeting with Jack I was itching to ask for an autograph but thought it wasn't the professional thing to do. Even as I left Danny's dressing room I regretted not asking for the autograph but never said a word to anyone.

I have no explanation for what i am about to tell you. It must have been over twenty years later and I was clearing my attic room out when I come across an old VHS video of Francie and Josie at the Kings Theatre. Edinburgh. By this time dvds had replaced videos and I had not looked at this copy for some time. I don't know why but I opened the VHS video cover and out fell a black and white postcard photo of Jack Milroy signed – 'To Steve from

Francie, Jack Milroy.' I still have the photo but how it got into the VHS I'll never know.

Moving on, in 2001 I came back to the UK after a long stint of cruising which had taken me to some great parts of the world I might never have seen any other way. I had really enjoyed my time of cruising but it was time to come back to Britain to set up home with my second wife Tracy. In November I had a call from Ian Liston who was the managing director of the Hiss & Boo Company. Ian toured his music hall show and always seemed to do the classier dates including Theatre Royal Windsor, Theatre Royal Bath, Swansea Grand and others. Most of the Music Halls would be topped by artistes like Danny La Rue, Roy Hudd, Ray Allen, Dora Bryan, Hinge and Bracket and so on.

Over the years Ian always included me on his bills and I always looked forward to working with this classy actor manager of the theatre. This time Ian's call was not in connection with a Music Hall date but concerning a pantomime at the Hall for Cornwall Truro starring the brilliant dancer Wayne Sleep as Dame. Ian asked if I was free which I was and asked again if I would be prepared to play comic opposite Wayne Sleep. I said that would be absolutely fine as long as I would have an opening spot and decent billing. I heard Ian stumble a bit before he said, "Oh yes, well I was meaning to tell you about that bit ... as it is November and so late we will not have time to actually put you on the bill.

I do not know to this day why a comic was not included on the bill, but I was glad to sign the contract. I played Jester against Wayne's Dame Trot, Wayne also directed the pantomime. The first day of rehearsals Wayne had an extra bit of script in his hand which he read out loud" it was in fact a full transcript of my variety act! I sat there in disbelieve until Ian Liston ran on stage and snatched the extra script out of Wayne's hand! I just looked on and wondered what that was all about.

I was very impressed with Wayne Sleep as a director and a person. He had no star edge to him at all, just a great chap full of energy. I remember one day in rehearsals Wayne flew into the room in his oversized woolly pullover and jeans and announced that there were some 'changes' to the script! Everyone gasped as it was day four of a scheduled six days of rehearsal... he then threw his script into the air and Roy Hudd's pristine script was just drifting in space. Then Wayne turned to me and said, "Steve, we have to dance, love. That's what I do!"

It was obvious that he had thought about this all night and not had that much sleep. He went on to say, "OK, no messing around now. I want you Steve and both ends of Daisy the Cow here now!" So we stood eagerly awaiting our next command. Wayne then went on to show the Cow and myself the dance steps and moves he required. Then he thought better of it and said, "Steve, show me ANY dance moves you can do, love!"

I went through some old variety steps I'd learnt from Ronnie Parnell. Wayne retorted. "Is THAT all?" I replied, "Yes that's it Wayne."

"OK," said Wayne and added. "With that last step where you travelled across stage to stage left, can you go the other way?

"No,"I replied.

Wayne tutted and then said, "No problem. Here we go..."

Inside ten minutes he had devised a choreographed dance routine that really worked both for the Cow and for me. My wife, Tracy, came to see the show and commented, "My goodness you're so clever, being able to dance so well." It was nice to hear of course, but it was all down to the genius of Wayne Sleep.

That season I did my 'Panto Rap' as an opening spot and stopped the show. So much so I was asked to come back by popular demand and play Widow Twanky the next year.

So next year I was appearing in Aladdin as Widow Twanky with Rick Wakeman' as Abanazar which was the most enjoyable panto I've ever done. To work with this great musical legend playing Abanazar to my Widow Twanky I loved every minute. Every day Rick would say to me, "What are we doing today Tanks?" His meaning was simply to ask what extra gags will we do. Although Rick was undoubtedly the star of the show he let me have full reign on the comedy, it was a great panto season smashing all box office records at the Hall for Cornwall Truro.

They always say that you should never regret the past so this memory is not seriously regretful rather than cringe worthy! As a newly elected water rat, Rick asked if I would be interested in doing a spot on a charity Gala show he organised during that panto season. I was happy to oblige and it soon came to pass that Rick had put a bill together with Stan Boardman, Paul Boardman and a few others. That night I'm in the wings and there's a definite buzz as Rick hosted this sell out charity show. This is the cringe-worthy bit … I spotted a young woman in the wings who was pacing to and fro and to me seemed a bit nervy. I felt sorry for her because I thought this is all must be new to her, a newcomer to the business. I went over to console her and said. "Hi … big breaths love, big breaths, you'll be alright.".

I cpould have fallen through the floow when I suddenly heard from the stage Rick announcing – "And now our special guest stars who are just back from an international tour. Here they are, Walking On Sunshine – Katrina and the Waves!!!!!! Even now I cringe at my words of encouragement for this international rock star.

CHAPTER FIFTEEN

Odd People And Superstitions

Entertainers are a breed all of their own whether they be singers, actors, dancers, comedians, acrobats, you name it. They don't quite fit in with the rest of society. Their outlook on life is different and in many ways that is why some show business people can never fully integrate with the rest of the world even if they have retired.

There are some false images though. For instance whenever a film has been made about circus you can pretty well guarantee that the clowns are always in make-up and the other artistes are always in their make-up. It doesn't matter what time of the day or night, whether it is a murder scene, a fire breaking out or simply a blizzard. The show people ae always filmed in costume. It isn't like that at all.

Artistes turning up at the theatre's stage door just look like ordinary people until they get inside and transform themselves into stage performers.

I remember someone telling me that they went to see a particular star performing at the White Rock Pavilion in Hastings. He took his wife with him and they approached the venue fairly early because the gentleman concerned needed to speak to the manager. As they approached they saw a rather shabby old chap looking at a notice board just outside.

The wife looked at him and felt sorry for him. "That old chap looks like he would be pleased to go inside and see the show but I doubt he can afford a ticket. Is there anything you can do?"

The man laughed and told her, "He's the star we've come to see!"

I'd better not tell you that the old man was actually the brilliant but, sadly, late Frankie Howerd who was not one who believed in 'dress to impress'.

On the subject of comedy, why is it tha most people seem to think that if you are a comedian or a clown you must, by nature, be miserable? Some are, of course, but that is not a comedy thing, that is simply a people thing.

If you were in the dressing room or at the Water Rats lodge meetings and heard the laughter you would never doubt that the idea that you have to be miserable to be funny is a complete myth.

Nerves can be a bit of a problem for many. There are legendary accounts of Des O'Connor fainting before appearing at the Glasgow Empire and some artistes are physically sick before going out in front of an audience. Still others have a drink before they perform. Sadly some drink a bit too much and I have seen some great performers fail to be at their best simply because they had a drink too many and messed up their act.

One night at the London Palladium a very popular comedy star became quite abusive towards his audience and 'died' a death. It tarnished an otherwise great reputation. Fortunately he got a grip after that and his next performance was a winner once again.

You would never see the greats like Ken Dodd, Norman Wisdom or Max Bygraves taking a drink for courage before they worked. They kept their focus on giving the audience the best night of its life and that was enough for them to be able to deliver.

Entertainers can be very superstitious though and some of the lengths they go to are quite amazing.

The wearing of green is never very popular on stage or in circus. It happens, of course, but if something goes wrong, invariably it will be the wearing of green by someone in the show that is likely to be blamed.

Wild birds flying around a circus tent is an omen of doom and gloom for the show. The performing parrots or pigeons are fine but a wild pigeon means that there is a disaster waiting to happen.

Ladies in a circus audience who are seen to be knititng are asked to stop as that is also considered to be very unlucky.

It easy to dismiss those things but you do get some strange tales.

A circus was appearing in Essex and the billers were taking posters round shops and giving tickets for the first performance to shop keepers who were willing to help. One lady who owned an antique shop was very helpful and allowed a poster in each window. She declined the free tickets though and explained that when she was living in Devon she had allowed circus posters in her shop and accepted the free tickets. She went to the performance which she was thoroughly enjoying until a lady fell from the trapeze and was badly injured.

The biller convinced her that lightning doesn't strike twice in the same way and she took the tickets and attended the performance. Yes, you've guessed it – a young lady fell from the trapeze and was badly injured.

In theatre there are many other superstitions. In pantomime for instance, the fairy always enters from stage right and the villain from stage left.

What about this one – when speaking, the panto fairy shoujld transfer her wand from her right hand to her left to protect her heart from evil. Yes, really.

It is also generally thought that the best way to court disaster for any panto would be to do the unthinkable and leave out the audience refrain: "It's behind you. Oh no it isn't. Oh yes it is."

Fresh flowers should never be seen on stage, except a bouquet at the end; a superstition invented, it is thought, by skinflint producers.

People are sometimes alarmed when they hear a performer say to another, "Break a leg." It is a way of saying 'good luck' without saying it as it is considered to be unlucky. Break a leg is not quiter as brutal as it sounds because its origins – and there are many versions – is said to be from the Elizabethan era when taking a bow was also spoken of as 'breaking a leg' meaning to bend the knee.

If you ever go into a theatre when it is empty you may find that there is a single light left on. This is known as the 'ghost light' and is said to keep the mischievous sp[irits away when there is nobody there. Another explanation is that it helps the first one in the building to find the main light switch!

Never use the word 'Macbeth' out loud. Oops, I think I used it but let's hope nobody noticed. It is thought to invoke evil and cause a curse on the production. There is a cure – the person saying it has to leave the theatre, spin round three times, spit and utter a Shakespearean curse (or a modern one if a Shakespearean one doesn't come readily to mind). So that's alright then.

A disaster during the dress rehearsal is not always a bad thing as the superstition goes that the opening performance will be very successful. Don't ask me, I'm only tellng you what is said.

Whistling in the theatre is also considered to be likely to bring bad luck and anyone caught is also likely to be told to go out and spin round three times before being allowed back into the venue.

Sleeping with the script under your pillow is another strange one. It is said to help you learn the lines better but I'm not quite sure how that works.

Finally, here's a ticklish one. Peacock feathers are thought to bring bad luck if they are used on stage. It is something to do with the 'eye' pattern which is thought to bring the 'evil eye' on the production.

I have heard that real money should never be used on stage but I think that is more to do with the bad luck brought upon the person who providses the money as there is a reasonable chance they won't see it again!

I am pleased to say that I have never been one to take these superstitions seriously. I take them all with a pinch of salt – er, that is to say that it has never done me any harm – touch wood!

CHAPTER SIXTEEN

Then And Now

Have you found that time flies these days? It is not just confinced to the entertainment world but somehow we all seem to have less time than we used to. I did think that it was because in our business you are always planning ahead. Not long after a new year has started you are getting the next festive season sorted and around about autumn you are often asked about the following summer. So it isnot just that there are often not enough hours in the day but what you thought you did just a few weeks ago was actually a decade or more.

In the 1990s I was asked to do a summer season in Whitby by the well known partnership of Trafford and Parnell. The company was run by two great stalwarts of variety. Tommy Trafford was a Lancashire comedian and dame and Ronnie Parnell a song and dance man. Tommy had suffered a few heart attacks, one of which was whilst he was playing Dame in one of his own productions. Now Ronnie Parnell just oozed showbiz, That's all he talked about. He loved it and dreamed of one day going back to the heyday of variety.

To give you an idea of the drive these fellows had, Tommy was taken to hospital between shows and the medical team diagnosed the heart attack. Ronnie asked the doctor to give Tommy an injection so that he could play the matinee! Tommy was a great Lancashire comic doing sketches and clean routines for seaside and panto audiences and when I was asked to deputise for him I considered it to be a great honour in more ways than one.

Firstly I was deputising for this great theatre comic and secondly

I'd never played top comic so this was a very big deal for me. The show needed three different changes of programme so I was a little nervous on opening night. Before we got that far though there were rehearsals and there was a comedy impressionist who was to support me on the bill. He was the very talented Mark Baylin.

I was expected to bring my own sketches to the show but had never done a sketch of my own in my life. On the weeks up to the summer season I had travelled to Llandudno to see one of the Trafford and Parnell shows at the old Grand Theatre/. It starred comic Don Reid. I spoke to Don about my concerns over having no sketches of my own, without hesitation he produced a copy of a sketch called 'Rich Man Poor Man'. I couldn't thank him enough – and still do.

So during rehearsals this sketch was put into the show and went like this:–

Tabs open showing a deckchair with posh towel over the back. A man walks out in shorts holding a large expensive beach umbrella and a nice bag. Clearly he is the rich man. Then I walk out with a carrier bag and an old battered umbrella. The rich man pulls out a copy of the Times and says into the wings (as if talking to his wife), "Oh look Daphne, our shares have rocketed – ha ha ha!!" The poor man pulls out a copy of the Dandy and says into the wings, as if talking to his wife, "Eee Beryl this Desperate Dan's funny tha knows." These exchanges go on like for like … i.e. smoked salmon and caviar sandwiches – jam butties – wine – water etc. until the rich man shouts into the wings, "Daphne come and join me'!" Out comes man in Drag (Mark Baylin).

Poor man says "Hey Beryl come on't beach its grand." out comes show girl with hips swinging. Poor man says, "Beryl you've left your engine running." A blackout signifies the end of the sketch. On paper it is just a script but in front of an audience it worked beautifully.

I was given a few other sketches by Ronnie one called The Photographer sketch and another called The Rose sketch but these were complicated in that a lot of other people were involved so unless they had comic timing they became a bit of a labour for me although we were still one sketch short which was a bit of a dilemma. What was I going to do?

The director was an absolute gem to me as he was also a working act , although he was getting a little testy as I'd been saying for days, "Oh. I'll run the last sketch by you soon."

We did a Music Hall for two nights, a Variety Show for two nights and a comedy farce written by Ronnie called One Yank And They're Off.

All during rehearsals Mark Baylin seemed to be shadowing me and one day he finally came to me and said, "I notice that you're doing Max Miller in the music hall show. I do Max Miller so why don't we do a double?"

In my mind I could not believe what I'd heard ... what a stupid idea that was I thought. I pulled rank a bit and retorted, "Oh no I don't think so." To be honest I had to find enough comedy material for six spots while Mark only needed to find enoigh for two spots. Max Miller was a precious four minutes to me and I needed it. I was certainly creative on that season and went back to my caravan every night trying to write jokes and routines for the next day's rehearsal. Well you don't want to look stupid do you?

So back to the last sketch. I'd asked Mark if he could impersonate Windsor Davies. He told me he could and have me an example whch was really very good OK. I was delighted ad suggested that he should go to the costume skip and see if he could find an army uniform or go to the Army and Navy store and get himself something from there, making sure to bring the receipt back. I went to the skip and found a pair of Khaki shorts and a pith Helmet and some army boots. With the addition of my white vest Id' created quite a good Don Estelle lookalike, not realising that this was to be a very important 'character' in my later career.

So the day comes when I must show the director the new sketch which I had not yet written! The dancers are rehearsing and it's nearly time for the dress rehearsal. I took Mark Baylin to one side and said, "Right Mark, you walk on as Windsor Davies and do some Windsor Davies patter. You are looking for me. I come on, we swap a few gags and then into the song 'Whispering Grass'. Hopefully there will be some apllause and then we exit."

147

That's when I found out that some impressionists, because they are locked in character, tend to over-think what they are doing. Mark pleaded, "Oh I can't just walk on and make it up Steve." I thought to myself, 'Don't give me problems just get on with it.' As the 'diplomatic ambassador' for Whitby I replied, "OK, just walk on and say something like. 'Welcome to the camp concert ... where's lofty' ......then I'll come on. You ask me where I've been. I tell you I've been to the chemist or doctors and you then say, 'What happened then?' I'll do the rest of the gag and then say something like 'Oh I went into this café or I went home' and that will lead into another gag."

By this time poor Mark's turning into a wreck. He was shaking and his face was going red. He said, "Yes but what's the cue for the song?" I replied, "Oh I'll just count the band in – it'll be alright.". I suppose on that occasion we were just two opposites – oil and water. My way seems to be a strange method to some theatre types I guess. At its best it is pure improvisation. The final result was that that particular sketch brought the house down. It came to be the highlight of the show ... and got longer and longer!

That summer season came to an end and by October I was doing club dates again and waiting for the phone to ring. Eventually it did.

It must have been a good 15 years after the panto with Frank Carson and Roy Barraclough at the Charter Theatre in Preston, that Duggie Chapman rang me. Ihad not long finished the summer season for Trafford and Parnell at Whitby.

Duggie asked me what my act was at the moment. I was still doing clubs but had been fortunate to secure the Whitby gig. I just said, "Oh this and that." Duggie replied, "I hear you do Max Miller and Tessie O'Shea?" I told him I did and I was duly booked by Duggie to do a gig at Grange-over-Sands. I am very grateful to be able to that I paralysed them – thank goodness. It had not been easy and took me about 40 mins to do it – but we got there in the end.

Later I was booked by Duggie for a summer season in Skegness and Southport. This time though we agreed on length of spots and so on so I didn't have to play it by ear as I had at Grange-over- Sands.

The audiences that Duggie's music hall shows attracted were far different from the clubs in that firstly it had to be clean and you had to register in the first 30 seconds as the spots were only around 12 mins. That is one of the lessons for anyone doing my kind of work – you have to be adaptable. You cannot have a one-size-fits-all act.

I then toured with Duggie's shows for the next 30 years. If Duggie liked what you did he kept you on! I had lots of adventures with Duggie as he was a likeable rogue and taught me lots of stuff I would never have learned in clubs. One of the best bits of advice was 'always do your strongest spot first' then you have the audience for the rest of the show.

Both Duggie and Beryl Johnson, his partner, once sat me down in Duggie's Jaguar and gave me a master class in communication with the audience. As I'm from Lancashire I was working the gags in a strong Lancashire accent – for warmth – which worked in Lancashire and Yorkshire but elsewhere they could not understand me! Duggie suggested that instead of 'Hav not bin well' I should change to change to, 'I've not been very well' still Lancashire but understandable to all!

I applied this advice to everything I said and it worked so thank you Duggie.

I was so lucky to meet Duggie as he introduced me to lots of old pros including Jacko Fossett whom I have mentioned before and his lovely wife Connie.

There will always be a special place in my heart for Duggie Chapman – he believed in me!

Or was I just working cheap at the time!

Duggie would ring me often giving me the dates for tours and panto plus all the showbiz gossip as he puffed on his cigar. One day in 1993 we were sharing a dressing room in , Stan Sennett's old theatre. Duggie gave me my cheque and said, "We can't go on like this Steve. Today we've only had 60 people in. We need a star name for our show."

He went on about who could top the bill while still puffing at his cigar. He said, "You see Frankie Vaughan's too poorly these days, Harry Secombe just does Songs of Praise, Danny La Rue would be great in this ...he loves all this Music Hall stuff." I buted in ands said, "Well why don't you ask him? Duggie just burst into laughter through his cigar smoke and said, "Ask him! He would not be interested in doing a show like this!" I insisted, "Well what have you got to lose, why don't you try?"

Duggie thought for a minute but the next I heard he was meeting Danny at the Birmingham Hippodrome. It was all a bit hush hush until one day he rang me and said, "OK Steve, brace yourself I've got a few dates for you. We start at the Bath Theatre Royal I'm putting everything I've got into this – the top of the bill is Danny La Rue!"

I was delighted, of course. The first date came and I was nervously looking forward to meeting someone I'd seen on stage and television who I never thought I'd meet let alone work with. As it turned out we got on like a house on fire. Later I wrote songs and sketches for Danny. My Mum had been to a clairvoyant once in the 70s who predicted that a tall man with white hair would boost my career, at the time we hoped it would be Hughie Green with his Opportunity Knocks TV show but it wasn't. Could Danny be that tall man with white hair?

Being on that first tour was like dream. Everyone in showbiz was talking about the show, it was packing theatres that had not been full since the old variety days. We played the Kings Theatre Southsea for a week, sometimes twice a day and they had to dust down benches in the gods. The tour was phenomenal. There I was working some of the best theatres in the UK with standing ovations every night – Birmingham Hippodrome, Kings Theatre Glasgow, Swansea Grand, Liverpool Empire.

Duggie could not believe his luck – he'd struck pure gold. We did tours for a good number of years and summer seasons in Blackpool, Bournemouth, Yarmouth. It was the best experience of my life and I can only thank Duggie Chapman and the tall man with the white hair – Danny La Rue.

One of my very favourite shows I've worked on was Four For The Road for Johnny Mans Productions. This also starred Danny

La Rue with support from yours truly, Donna Mayers and Danny Owen. We had a great live band led by David Carter on keys, Franny Heywood on drums and John Armitage on bass guitar.

At the time Danny was on top form. He must have been in his 60's but he had all his glamour with an absolute razor sharp wit and a personal assistant called Annie Galbraith. We had a great opening where every one introduced Danny and then we took turns singing parodies of Lady is a Tramp, Let me Sing a Happy Song and so on.

I had two spots – one in the first half and another in the second. I had toured with Danny before as I have just mentioned so I was very comfortable with the show which was a touring 1994 summer season with a string of dates starting with Skegness Embassy Theatre then down to Ilfracombe Pavilion, up to Western Super Mare's Playhouse Theatre then up further to Llandudno. Duggie had left me a card as he was at the Embassy on the first Sunday. The card read, 'All the best mate and do your best spot first!" It was a nice gesture – once again.

For this show I had made a Gladstone bag for the props in the act with legs that fell out of the bottom. At the time the act went like this – Danny would introduce me as – 'please welcome that bungle of fun – Steve Barclay!'

Out I came with a long fur coat and carrying my Gladstone bag as if looking for somewhere to park it then down came the legs. I took off the fur coat revealing a bright purple suit, wafted the fur coat and talcum powder came out of it to look like dust. I dropped it to the floor then shot it with a starting pistol and it flew off into the wings. Then I went into the gags and comedy zany impressions finishing with Ken Dodd.

One day we were traveling to the IOM to play Gaiety Theatre with Danny and I'd put the starting pistol in my uke case. When I went through security the police came and I was taken away to be searched and grilled. I missed the Matinee which put me and everyone else into a panic and then when I did arrive at the theatre Danny in full make up just said, "You little fool" or words to that effect!

We became firm friends during those tours and concerts. Danny always gave good advice and a place on his shows right to the end. Once we were playing the Leeds City Varieties together and after the show both Dan and I had more than our share of champagne. As we sat at the back of the circle Dan slurred 'you know luv this is my theatre'. To which I replied in an equally slurred voice but this time in his voice 'I know Dan'. Dan laughed from bottom of his seat and said, "Just a minute – I'm me, you're not me. Goodness Steve you've got me tipsy again!"

Some time later i made what was to be my last call to Danny. I said, "Hello Dan, how are you mate?" His voice was shallow which seemed so strange for him. Danny replied, "Oh Steve, I've felt better luv." I never spoke to Danny again. A few weeks later he passed away. I had lost a great mentor, a great friend and of course, my tall man with white hair.

Life went on of course but there has always been an empty spot on the stage where Danny once stood.

My work is still varied and I have continued playing Dame in pantomimes and being Steve Barclay the rest of the time. There seems to be a trend in theatres these days to use 'over-camp' Dames. I wonder if this is because managements don't really know how a traditional dame works? Or, in their minds, are they modernising? The only ones that come close for me are Eric Potts and Christopher Biggins. I do hope the gag is not lost in time. Basically the Dame is exactly as I have said before, not a drag queen but a clown dressed as a woman. The best Dames are are comics first and panto dames as a result.

I had a strange experience quite recently which possibly demonstrates a new approach to panto and, perhaps, entertainment in general. I was working in a pantomime at one of my old haunts, the Playhouse Theatre, Weston Super Mare and was thrilled to see my photo still in the green room. This was from the time of the touring summer season – Danny Goes to Hollywood – for Dave Ballinger of Barron Knights fame.

That was in the 1990s but now we are talking about a 2019 production of Cinderella which starred Linda Lusardi. Linda's hubby Sam Kane directed it and played one of the ugly sisters. I was booked to play Baron Hard up a new venture for me as i was usually the Dame.

These days everything is high tech including communication with agents, producers and directors. About September Sam Kane rang me and we had a very delightful conversation about the forthcoming panto that Sam was to direct while also writing the script. He didn't know me, and I didn't know him at this point, but I found him to be a real down to earth scouser.

During our long conversation Sam suggested I sing and play my ukulele in the first half of the show and asked if I had anything else to offer. We both agreed that I should walk on playing the uke, do a short song then go into something I've done for a long time called The Panto Rap. I had sent Sam audio clips of my Panto Rap as well as PDF transcripts etc., so he knew where he was with it. I'm all for keeping spots in theatre productions tight so it ran in total four minutes. I'd made up a very short parody of Cleaning Windows – which I named I've Got Money Troubles – just to get on. I'd thought in advance about getting the ukulele off stage by passing it into the wings whilst I said, "Take that back to Cash Converters will you" then two gags and into The Panto Rap and finish.

I'd emailed all this to Sam. word for word, so he could copy it into his panto script. After a while the full script finally arrived and there it was: Enter Baron. uke ditty and into Panto Rap. I'd been told by Sam that there was a live band to play for the show, so I emailed all the musical arrangements in advance plus backing tracks for rehearsals or reference. The reason for my attention to detail was that I've been in so many pantos and I've watched directors under pressure. I thought if I could arrive with my spot already rehearsed ready to go it would help everyone including Sam.

Finally, the first day of rehearsals arrived and I met Linda and Sam plus the other cast members including Joe Rowntree who was to play Buttons, a very nice young fella I thought to myself. This was Joe's first pantomime and he had a big part as Buttons. Although it was only the first day of rehearsals, I'd brought along my uke just to be safe because you never know during rehearsals when the 'spots' will be rehearsed. It wasn't needed of course but as the old gag goes – 'it was there if you wanted it'.

The other cast members and the band who were all early twenties must have thought I was from planet zonk as certain things I said went straight over their heads, I was as they say 'out of my comfort zone' but this time on the wrong side of it. I was amazed when I said to Sam when we do the 'tie up' etc, He replied. "Tie up? What's that'?

On Day Two I was asked to perform my spot by Sam. I did it dry (that means without the band). Sam laughed at my gags and applauded my uke ditty and Panto Rap. The rest of the young cast and Linda congratulated me. By day three Joe and I were struggling with one of the gags in the show which wasn't a panto gag at all it was merely a steal of an old Abbot and Costello sketch. It went something like 'Mr. What's in the first house, Mr.Who's in the second house and Mr.Why is in the third house'. To which Joe said, 'But who's in the first house.' I then said, 'No, What's in the first house' etc.

To do this right it needed to be done at record speed...the truth was neither of us believed in the gag. The pace was laboured and intermittent, so it was decided to cut it! I would have just loved to take Joe through a proper traditional panto gag. He has the talent but alas it wasn't to be.

In my early pantos the MD started playing on an upright piano in the corner with a fag in his mouth and a fag burning in the ashtray from day one. Now it seems bands including MDs seem to have other things to do like connecting wires and speakers etc. However, it's now day five and we are running all of the first half including spots.

Sam had already asked me to be in the 12 days of Christmas song to which I confirmed I was up for it. During my spot the band didn't play so they used the tracks (which were very good and created by Alan McPike a Scottish jazz musician. the best in the business). Yet again the spot went over great with the other cast members and those watching. Just one drawback. This time Sam Kane wasn't laughing and looked at me very strangely from under the lids of his eyes.

After the rehearsal Sam shouted from his director's seat in the church hall where we were rehearsing and said, "Steve we need to cut the spot down a bit."

"Okay," I replied and added, "Let's do a proper cut." Sam (thinking I was going the extra mile here) lsaid, "Let's cut the uke song plus two gags." I was happy to do this as less is best and it was a prop I didn't need. This was a savage cut by me making a four-minute spot into two minutes. But then Sam said we need to cut the rap down as well, to which I replied, "No Sam. the Rap works. I've done it a million times before and it's honed and polished to two minutes. If you want me to cut this I will but it will not be tampered with!" Sam said, "Okay let's cut it." Then I knew what the funny look in his eye was as I went through the spot, with everyone else in stiches.

The other cast members gasped when the cut was announced. It was replaced with the Twelve Days of Christmas which was ten minutes long and done at the wrong tempo. The correct tempo for this type of comedy is 6/8 marching tempo. Needless to say, I wasn't invited to be in it, but for the first time in my panto career the Fairy God Mother Linda Lusardi was happy to be in it and do pratt falls every night!

The moral of the story is that there are still some wise and esxperienced heads in this business but many people prefer to see them on a pike rather than admit that they usually know best.

CHAPTER SEVENTEEN

Comedy Turns

L ife goes on and is the usual rollere-coaster ride that is the usual path of anyone involved in show business. Just when you are biting your nails over what work isn't coming in, one phone call can make a massive difference. By the same token you can be thrilled to bits to start a lengthy season only to find that there is nothing else at the end of it – for a while at least.

That is why many entertainers have taken to putting their own shows together and promoting it themselves. You kind of hope that someone wll see it and want the show – or you – for their venue, cruise or whatever. At the very least you are doing something positive. The worst thing for an entertainer is to be doing nothing except waiting for the phone to ring. Even if you are a star name, you are easily and quickly forgotten.

Also, if you are the sort of person that likes to be doing something all the time you are driven to make something happen. There are only so many times you can cut the grass, fix the plumbing or visit a garden centre. I like making props and costumes but there has to be a point in it.

That is why I have taken to putting my own shows together – variety shows, music hall, wartime shows – you name it. I always make sure they are flexible enough to go to any sort of venue and they have ticked over nicely. My priority is always, to perform in other people's shows but I am pleased that my own productions have also worked.

One in particular has been very popular – Comedy Turns!

I devised this as a real departure from what I usually do.

Originally I created this as a one-man drama with some assistance from an old ventriloquist dummy's head! Unlike many one-man plays which run for about an hour and have something else in support, this one ran for the full evening and regularly played to an average 85% audience. One newspaper write up said that the audience, "was simply spellbound, standing as one at the end to acclaim this excellent production." That is a real feel-good factor and makes the journey home so much better.

The Comedy Turns one man play was set in a dressing room with the character Johnny Rainbow, an old comic and pantomime dame, preparing for a performance. As he goes through the routine of make-up, costume and so on his life flashes before him with all its ups and downs, delights, disappointments and disasters. Sometimes hilarious, sometimes painful you can never be absolutely sure if he is going to get out there on stage or end it all in the dressing room.

This was indeed a new challenge for me. As you may have read earlier in the book I had been around for some years as comic, impersonator, singer and comedy actor. This time I exposed another layer of my questionable talent with clever writing, a great concept and tremendous on-stage presence.

All that sounds great, but it was the on stage presence that caused a problem. I have mentioned before that much of my act is ad-lib. I have a routine but I am not one of those who cannot stray outside the well-rehearsed performance. I like to throw in gags on the spur of the moment, react to the audience and so on. That actually caused me a problem with Comedy Turns, I could never stick to the actual script. With a play you really have to even if you are the only one performing it and have written it in the first place.

So after touring with Comedy Turns as a one man play I decided to rewrite it as a one man show. When I toured Comedy Turns as a play the audience seemed to enjoy me coming out of character and doing the comedy routines, like Max Miller, Tessie O'Shea, Ken Dodd and the rest of the many stars. So I decided to take trhe plunge and re-invent Comedy Turns.

It evolved as the perfect vehicle for me. The opening is not what you would expect and involves the audience from the beginning to the end. I go through the Music Hall and variety acts of the past explaining the term 'Billing matter' 'Five and nine' and many of the other sayings and quirks of the entertainment world that rarely stray from behind the scenes.

During the summer of 2019 I took the show to the Neverland Theatre in Skegness. About ten minutes before curtain up the owner of the theatre, Gary Starr, came in the dressing room and mentioned that eight young men had booked to see it thinking it was alternative comedy. He was worried that they might not like it.

I was a bit concerned too but not too much. Naturally I was very aware of their age and probable conceptions of what a comedy show is but we need not have had any worries. Those young chaps loved it and I suppose to them it was sort of alternative because they thought Max Miller was the eighties comic who did the Noddy routine mistaking him for Mick Miller.

I actually enjoy performing Comedy Turns because there's only me in it I can virtually do anything I want – comedy, swing, jazz what ever the room requires. That's the secret really being able to read a room and change accordingly, something I learned to do in cabaret clubs many years ago.

Comedy Turns can be adapted to any format and is very easy to set up as theatre show, after dinner speech or cabaret which is why it has proved to be very popular with all kinds of venues, promoters, charities and so on.

Over the years I've done a number of one man shows but Comedy Turns stands out from the rest. For me it's such a breeze as I'm able to do my luverly jazz and swing songs. Something I could never do on a Duggie Chapman seaside show! When I started a new show, my favorite part was always the band call. I just love music and Comedy Turns allows me to perform songs like Lady Is A Tramp, Anything But Love, plus one of my very favourites, To Be With You. I even do a tribute to the great George Melly and have written a parody about George. Rather than just stand there and say 'and now my tribute to George Melly' I just sing about him in my parody of This Joint isJjumping.

Yes, I'm quite pleased with Comedy Turns as it has evolved, I suppose it's rather like a suit that fits well, you're comfortable in it!

I am pleased to say that the phone has never stayed silent for too long but I am delighted that I have Comedy Turns to take on the road should there be any gaps in my diary.

CHAPTER EIGHTEEN

Don't Be Shy – Take Courage!

From my very first production in a shed in Limeside with Torchy the Cat I've always loved Showbusiness. I've been fortunate to do everything I ever wanted to do, I just wanted to be in Showbusiness and do what I do best. Along this great journey I've been lucky to meet some wonderful seasoned pros of 'The Business' including many household names – and I don't mean Daz – if you're star struck.

Some of the greatest are the performers who you only know about if you're actually in the business. The first time I met Roy Earl a comedy magician from Coventry – correction a 'Mad Magician' from Coventry – was in 1977 the year Elvis died, and Roy and I were appearing in summer season at the Fort Regent, Jersey. During the rehearsal week we practiced at various hotels around the island.

One day Roy said to me, "Steve how will you get back to St Helier?" I replied, "Oh I'll get a taxi." Roy milked this to the full with just one word but several bizarre faces and looks of absolute horror, he exclaimed "TAXIE'!!!" as if I was stark raving mad. Every time we met afterwards, I reminded him of this wonderful gag.

The other time was when I called on him at his home in Swansea unexpected and he was sunbathing in the garden. He had no idea I was arriving as I crept up behind him to surprise him he opened one eye from his sleep and said, "Oh no! It's Steve Hutch from Fort Regent! Have I died and no one's told me."

These wonderful friends I have met along the way Andrew Van

Buren became a great friend from the Danny La Rue days. He taught me so much about the props I was using in the act and advised me how to refine them until they worked just right.

For me the funniest story has got to be when we were at the Theatre Royal, Bath with Danny La Rue. I hadn't known Andrew long and he hadn't known me long enough to realise that I was a bit of a practical jocker. We had been in the theatre since around 10.00 am by now it was around 1.30 and Andrew was a growing lad so by now was as hungry as a horse! He mentioned he was hungry to which I said well go and help yourself to a sandwich then. He replied, "A sandwich? Where?"

"Oh." I said quite casually. "At the stage door. They are complimentary and in a big cardboard box." Andrew was delighted to hear this and dashed down the steps to grab a sandwich. He came back with his morsel, but then said, "I'll tell you what Steve, the stage crew are giving me some funny looks." I replied. "I'm not surprised – you're eating their dinner." We always laugh about this even to this day when we meet on a show or at a Water Rats lodge.

We are always learning in this great business of ours and Tommy Cooper once advised me, 'Try and make use of every opportunity,' even if your dying the death. Learn from it and try to understand where you went wrong."

When you have a bad night and believe me, I've had them, it's not always the audience's fault, could it be that you just haven't delivered the goods as you should. I once did a cabaret in Brighton at the Max Miller appreciation society dinner. I made a big mistake halfway through I put a white trilby on and did a Max Miller routine. There must have been about twenty-five other Max Miller impersonators in the room. After my show Mike Leader who was a member looked at me and just shrugged his shoulders with a smile. But only a pro with a very kind heart like Brother Water Rat Jack Seaton would say, "Steve it wasn't you, it was the lighting."

There are still some great characters in show business like a great friend of mine – Freddie "Parrot Face" Davis. We traveled together to Chelsea masonic Lodge (only open to theatricals and musicians) and on the way back on the train he got out a scrap of paper and started writing ditties for me. It's the people like Freddie I'll never forget and I am so proud that they have been part of my life.

How surreal has this journey been. The first time I saw Freddie was whilst he was appearing in summer season in Blackpool. At that time I was watching him from a theatre seat and now here's that Steve Barclay fella sat beside him on a train to Kings Cross.

One of my greatest friends in showbusiness has got to be Rollo. I knew him when he worked as Reggie Mental. We first met in Benidorm working for an agent called George Williams. I think it must have been 1999 and I'd just finished a pantomime with Little and Large and Jess Conrad at Hanley Theatre Royal. Jess very kindly recommended me to the agent George Williams. George was then a typical Yorkshire agent; he rang me at my flat in Dawlish Warren, Devon.

"Hello," he said in a broad Yorkshire accent "It's George here ... Jess Conrad reckons you'd go down well at Gigolo's on the Benidorm comedy strip." He went on, "It's a luverly room and you can stay for six months! Just a nice little Cabaret spot about midnight for an hour, there's accommodation but no flights."

A week later I was on a flight to Benidorm to be met by Rollo and his 'luverly' family – Michelle his wife and only weeks old Lucy. We all got on like a house on fire, but on the way to the first gig that night something wasn't right. Rollo was hiding something, and I couldn't quite put my finger on it.

We chatted on the way and Rollo said, "Oh by the way, Steve Hewlett can't wait to meet you ever since he saw your name on the blackboard."

"Blackboard? "I quizzed him?"

"Well yes." Rollo replied and added, "But as George must have told you, 'It's a luverly room'."!

When we arrived, yes it was a luverly room ... indeed it was full of pillars clad in mirrors but it was one of the very worst you could imagine with passing trade. Everyone was drunk by 8.00 pm and there was a dressing room full of nervous comics dreading to be told. "You're on at midnight."

Rollo and I kept in contact and even now we call each other 'George' and always comment 'It's a luverly room'.

There are the new pros you'll meet with different name of course, if you're lucky enough to have bit of talent. If you take the plunge to embark on a showbusiness career these people will find you. So even if you just open the fridge the light comes on and you sing a chorus of 'That's Life' have a go! It's great to see young Tommy Rollason (Rollo's son) venturing into this great business of ours with his glamorous assistant Lucy his sister who was a babe in arms in Benidorm's 'luverley room. Since those days we have all done panto together, Water Rats shows and who knows? – This year we might just perform together again in yet another luverly room.

Some performers are courageous and, let's be honest, their bravery and self-confidence can make up for any deficiency in their talent. I have – we all have – seen entertainers who may even be the top-of-the-bill and you wonder how they ever got there. Usually they just have supreme courage and a belief in themslves, sopmetimes to the point of total arrogance and a refusal to listen to anyone who might possibly be able to offer a word of advice.

The real stars are those who don't actually see themselves as stars. They are the sort who will chat to you and have a cup of tea and, even though they are selling out all over the country, will say, "How do you think I could improve such and such?"

Then there are countless others who would love to have a go, perhaps have real talent but they are, by nature, shy and think very little of themselves or their talent.

I have often spoken to people like that and ask them why they don't at least try. I have heard many different answers but they all come down to the same thing.

Some say, "I'm just kidding myself.".

Others say, "I'm no good really, I can only do one song.".

Also there is, "Oh I couldn't do that, get up there in front of everyone?! No way."

Sadly there is also, "I thought about it but my Dad (or someone else) told me not to be so stupid."

The list goes on and on and I find it very sad indeed that there is so much real talent that is never actually allowed to blossom. It is like seeing a flower trampled on before it gets the chance to show us how great it is.

The world of entertainment has changed and will always change. Music for instance has changed. Back in the days gone by a band or group would be out once, twice or the times a week playing at weddings or other parts, maybe at a dance in the church hall or at a pub. They liked certain music themselves but had to learn to play and sing a ide selection because at a wedding the young ones would ask for the latest hit while grandad would want to join in and sing a favourite song from the way years. They really learned the trade and then one day an agent, manager or promoter would perhaps wander in and hear them and the next thing you knew they were in a recording studio, getting better gigs and able to consider going fully professional.

It rarely works like that today. The are boy 'bands' and girl 'bands' who cannot play an instrument between them. Often records are made by session people in a studio and then whoever is behind the project will start looking for suitable faces to fit the music. It has changed tremendously.

The general entertainment business has also undergone many changes with TV 'talent' shows set up just to make money for the few. There are many so-called comedians who seem to rely on bad language and subject matter to get a 'laugh'. It is a shame because some of those comics are brilliantly funny and don't need to throw in four letter words.

Live music has taken a bit of a bashing too. Every panto had a band and some a full orchestra in days gone by but today the economics of live entertainment mean that quite often there is no live music at all – not even someone with a kazoo!

The result is that backing tracks are used and so lip-synching (miming to you and me) has been added which means that it is possible for a 'recording artiste' to have a hit which was created without them ever having been in the recording studio and never having to sing it live.

What has all that got to do with you and your potential talent?

It is simply this – if you feel an extra buzz deep inside when you walk into a theatre, if you feel something welling up inside when you hear the applause of an audience, if you feel a constant nagging that tells you that you really want to express something whether in song, making people laugh, amazing them with a card trick or by dancing, juggling, falling on the floor or holding their attention as you read them a story – your talent is knocking on a locked door from the inside saying. "Will someone please let me out!"

You have the key in your hands – it is called 'courage'.

Don't be shy – use the key. You won't regret it and you might just enjoy it.

In writing this book I'd just like to thank all the wonderful people in my theatrical life, who have put up with my OCD condition of showbiz, insisting that the sound's right, the lighting right and so on.

There have been many people who have helped me with advice, contacts and door openings and I am grateful to each and everyone of them. I hope i have followed their wonderful examples and helped a few people myself along the way.

May I also say a huge thank you to my family for allowing me to live the dream and especially my wife, Tracy, for allowing me to fill her storage cupboards and an attic crammed with costumes props and sheet music. How she ever finds space to put any of the less important things like cups and saucers, I shall never know.

Have fun!

Steve Barclay
As Sir Ken Dodd.

Steve Barclay and family.

Steve Barclay as Lofty.

Steve's sons, Ashleigh and Elliot.

Steve at 17.

Billie and Trevor George.

*Steve Barclay –
cheeky chappie.*

Steve Barclay as A Dame.

Danny and friends.

Danny, Steve and Duggie.

Francie and Josie signed pic.

Grandson – Gruff.

Leeds CV chairman.

Les Dawson.

Mum and us.

Me as Me!

Steve portrait and inset,
Top of the bill.

PAVILION THEATRE
NEW ROAD, BRIGHTON

3.00pm | SUNDAY 22nd NOVEMBER 2009 | ONE PERFORMANCE ONLY

MAX MILLER APPRECIATION SOCIETY
proudly presents

VARIETY
SHOWTIME

Starring STEVE BARCLAY and his guests

PETE
LINDUP

ROLLO
The Entertainer

YVONNE
LLOYD

ROY HILTON
and his music

Tickets £16 from THE DOME BOX OFFICE
01273 709709
www.maxmiller.org

Water Rats gather.

Steve with Doddy.

Steve with jazz singer, Elaine Delmar.

Steve and just some of his showbiz pals.

Steve with John Inman.

Steve with long-suffering Tracy.

Steve with Ray Alan.

Steve and Rollo.

Steve with Ronnie Parnell.

*My daughter –
Bea.*

Youthful Steve.

Steve with Roy and Wyn Calvin.